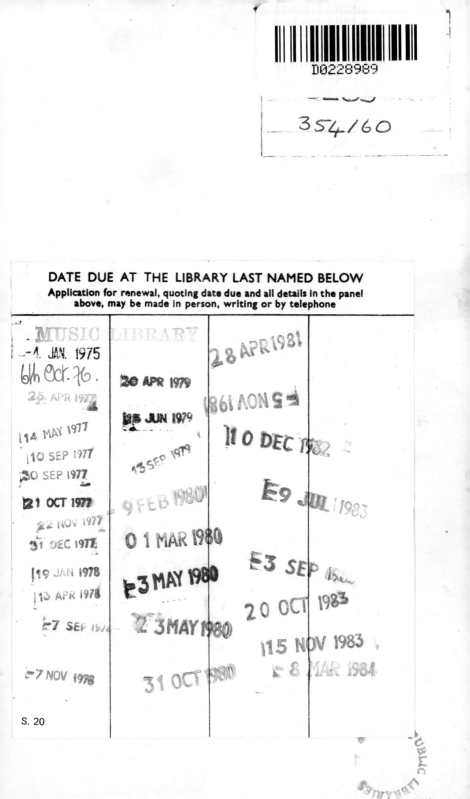

History of the Piano

History of the Piano

Ernest Closson

Translated by Delano Ames
Edited and revised by Robin Golding

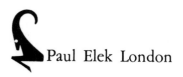

Paul Elek London

Originally published in 1947 in Great Britain
by Elek Books Ltd, this edition published in 1974
is completely updated and revised.

Elek Books Ltd
54-58 Caledonian Road
London N1 9RN

ISBN 0 236 17685 4

Printed by Weatherby Woolnough Ltd., Wellingborough,
Northamptonshire

Contents

List of Plates

Appendix

Preface to the Second Edition

Ernest Closson's *Histoire du Piano* was first published in 1944 by Éditions Universitaires, Brussels, and an English version, translated by Delano Ames, was published in London by Paul Elek in 1947. Closson (1870-1950) was for many years Curator of the Museum of the Conservatoire Royal in Brussels, which boasts one of the richest collections of keyboard instruments in the world, and he was therefore well qualified to write a book on their evolution. When his book first appeared the subject was poorly documented and the opportunities for seeing and hearing old keyboard instruments were extremely limited, but today interest in them is widespread and they are very much more accessible (and better cared for).

Although a number of important works on the subject have appeared in the meantime (notably those by Hirt, Boalch, Russell, and Hubbard, for details of which see Bibliography), it was felt that a revised edition of Closson's book would be of value. It is an excellent summary, clear and readable, of the piano and its antecedents. In revising the work I have tried to retain the flavour of the original, while at the same time incorporating emendations made by the author since the publication of the French and English editions, as well as corrections to the translation, and additional material made in the light of subsequent research and documentation. The original French edition carried a few line-drawings only; in the first English one these were supplemented by photographic reproductions of seventeen instruments. This new edition incorporates an almost completely new, and more representative, selection of photographs, several new diagrams of actions, and a considerably amplified bibliography. Some of the instruments described in the text were destroyed in the Second World War. Others have been shown, by recent research, to be rather less representative and interesting than those which have been illustrated in this new edition. The book's original title has been retained depite the fact that, as M. Closson explains in his Introduction, it deals in considerable detail with other stringed keyboard instruments besides the piano, notably the clavichord, the harpsichord, the spinet and the virginal.

Encouragement for producing a revised edition of Ernest Closson's book came from his son, M. Herman Closson, and I should like to acknowledge the enthusiasm he has shown in helping to bring this about. I also wish to thank Moira Johnston of Paul Elek for her patience and help in seeing this book through its various stages to press.

Robin Golding
1973

Introduction

The immense importance to music of the instrument on which the music is played has not always been sufficiently stressed. The instrument directly influences musical composition, conditions it and even inspires it, both by its capacities and by its limitations. In a sense the instrument creates musical style, marking out its stages of development, rather as his building material does for the architect. The invention of the Boehm system for the woodwinds and, still more, that of valves for brass instruments have in the last analysis an importance equal to that of the masterpieces which make use of them. Without these inventions the masterpieces themselves would be neither possible nor even conceivable. The theory of equal temperament inspired Bach to write one of the outstanding masterpieces of keyboard literature; the perfecting of the brass was the initial condition of the unlimited chromaticism and frenzied modulation of *Tristan und Isolde*.

Like the cithara in antiquity and the lute during the Renaissance, the piano is today our most important musical instrument. We could not imagine our musical life without it.

This importance it owes primarily to its harmonic and polyphonic capacities. Unlike the violin, a keyboard instrument is sufficient when played by itself; that is why after the lute was forgotten solo composition was concentrated first on the harpsichord then on the piano. A diminutive orchestra in itself, the piano generally refuses to associate with the orchestra except in the piano concerto where it plays the dominating part.[1]

On the other hand it is for the piano that the symphony itself is arranged – and what a satisfaction it is to 'read' with four hands in a free and spontaneous interpretation the works of the masters! The songs of Schubert, Schumann and Fauré are inconceivable without the piano. It is also the normal adjunct to musical creation; on its keys in the form of sketches, most symphonic works are born. But above all it is the piano which is the most usual interpreter of musical thought, its literature being greater in quantity, though not always in quality, than all other musical literature. It was enough to express the multiple genius of Chopin who thought only for and by the piano.

Most of our domestic music is supplied by the piano. With its delicacy of expression, which enables it to translate by means of the slightest gradations of tone the subtlest emotions, it showed itself capable and worthy, in those improvisations which his contemporaries thought superior even to his published work, of Beethoven's sublime meditation.

Interpreter of intimate thought and commonest domestic instrument, the piano dominates public musical life as well. Piano recitals are more numerous than all other kinds of musical performances. Halls devoted to piano recitals by piano manufacturers became centres of musical activity. Such are the Salle Pape, the Salles Dietz, Petzold, Erard and Pleyel in Paris, Bösendorfer in Vienna, Blüthner in Berlin, Steinway Hall and Chickering Hall in New York, where every year innumerable recitals take place in which the greatest virtuosos play. They have become the seat and centre of important artistic associations. We may quote here the eloquent, indeed impassioned lines written by Liszt, in a letter he addressed to the *Gazette musical* in Paris in 1838: 'Perhaps I am deluded by this mysterious feeling which binds me to the piano, but

---

[1] There exist but few symphonic works in which the piano is treated simply as an instrument in the orchestra on the same footing as other instruments: notably, Gounod's *Philémon et Baucis,* Saint-Saëns's Symphony in C minor, D'Indy's *Symphonie Cévenole,* Stravinsky's *Pétrouchka,* Honegger's *Jeanne d'Arc.* The reason for this is that the timbre of the piano blends poorly with the orchestra; it remains, as Lavoix says, 'insoluble'. Berlioz pointed out the fact in his *Grand traité d'instrumentation et d'orchestration modernes.* It had already been pointed out fifteen years previously by Fétis (in his *Curiosités historiques de la musique,* 1830) after that eminent musicologist had heard in London symphony concerts directed at the piano by Sir George Smart and Dr Crotch.

12

I regard its importance as enormous. To my mind, the piano occupies the highest place in the hierarchy of instruments: it is the one most widely cultivated, the most popular of all, and it owes this importance and popularity partly to the harmonic resources which it alone possesses, and, because of this, to its ability to epitomise and concentrate the whole musical art within itself. Within the compass of seven octaves it covers the spectrum of the orchestra, and the ten fingers of one man are enough to reproduce the sounds created by a hundred musicians in concert. It is thanks to the piano that we have an opportunity to become familiar with works that would otherwise be little known or completely unknown because of the difficulty of assembling an orchestra to perform them. It has the same relationship to orchestral music as engraving does to painting: it multiplies it and makes it available to all; and if it does not reproduce its colours at least it reproduces its light and shade.'

In the history of the piano which follows, we are far from pretending (nor was it our intention to attempt) to give a detailed and complete history of the instrument, its mechanism and all its forerunners, a task which would take many volumes and the technical aspects of which would quickly exhaust the reader. (A task of extreme difficulty, moreover, in view of the frequent impossibility of identifying the authentic inventor of such and such an improvement or the real innovator of this and that process, as builders cheerfully claimed as their own and even patented novelties which were often only 'borrowed'!) We have preferred to draw the broad outlines, to emphasise the chief stages of the instrument's history, to show the bonds and interchange between the principal centres of its manufacture, to point out the relationship between the instrument and the music written for it.

The history falls naturally into three parts: the Clavichord, the Harpsichord, the Spinet and the Virginal, and the Piano itself. A word of explanation concerning only the section at the end of Part 3, which deals with the mechanism of the piano: because of its purely technical character and the peculiar complexity of the piano we thought it best to give these details a special chapter instead of dispersing them throughout the text.

The book is dedicated to the memory of our master and predecessor Victor-Charles Mahillon, founder of the Musée du Conservatoire in Brussels, which he directed for forty-seven years and which, thanks to him, became the richest and most beautiful of all collections. We have seized this occasion to render a modest homage to the memory of this eminent man honoured by specialists throughout the world, and who, with his monumental five-volume *Catalogue du Musée instrumental du Conservatoire de Bruxelles,* was the founder of the modern objective science of musical instruments which he substituted for the purely bookish treatment the subject had received until then.

We wish to thank M. L. Anthonis, director of the Maison Günther, MM. G. and M. Hautrive, piano makers, M. S. Moisse, technician of the Musée du Conservatoire in Brussels, who helped us with their special knowledge of the instrument's mechanism, and finally M. Hoc, Curator of the Department of coins and medals in the Bibliothèque Royale, who furnished us with necessary information about the present value of old money.

Ernest Closson
1944

The following symbols are used to indicate notes throughout the range of instruments referred to in the book:

1 *The Clavichord*

A taut string can be vibrated in three different ways. It can be plucked with the fingers or a plectrum like the guitar, stroked with a bow like the violin, or struck with a mallet or hammer like the piano. The earliest form of stringed keyboard instrument, the clavichord, is struck; the next, the harpsichord with its derivatives, the virginal and the spinet, are plucked; and finally the piano, like the clavichord, is struck.

The prototype of all stringed instruments which are struck is the dulcimer (called in Italian *dolce melo*, in German *hackbrett*, and in French *tympanon*). It has existed since antiquity and is still played from the Near East to the Far East and by most of the peoples of Europe. Its most developed and artistic form may today be found in the Hungarian *cimbalom*, which will be familiar to anyone who has heard a Hungarian Gipsy orchestra. The dulcimer normally consists of a flat case, trapezoidal in shape, the sides narrowing as the strings grow shorter. The strings run parallel with its base and pass over two bridges fixed to the soundboard. They are struck by two small mallets held one in each hand.

We do not know precisely where or when someone first thought of

15

the idea of replacing this method of hand percussion with a keyboard mechanism, though it appears to have been before the fourteenth century. Organ keyboards had existed in a rudimentary form (at first purely diatonic) since the twelfth century[1], and in the thirteenth century had already been greatly improved. We are not sure what the original name of the new stringed instrument was[2]. Possibly it was the *echiquier* or *schachbrett*, which appear quite frequently in ancient texts. The instrument was also called the *monochord* or the *manicordion*, from the Latin *monochordium*, which was in antiquity an instrument of scientific experiment, fitted with a single string the length of which could be varied by the pressure of the finger or by a movable bridge. In the second century the Greek scientist Ptolemy replaced the single string by a series of fifteen, representing a double diatonic octave.

Though it had thus become a *multi*chord the instrument continued during the Middle Ages to be called a *monochordium*. According to Schaeffner's hypothesis (in the article *Clavecin* in the *Encyclopédie de la musique et Dictionnaire du Conservatoire de Paris*) the monochord had by then become the *manicordion* or *manicorde*, and when finally furnished with a keyboard the *clavichord* (Latin, *clavichordium*; Italian, *clavicordo*; French, *clavicorde*). The word clavichord appears for the first time in 1404, in the rules for Minnesingers drawn up by Eberhard Cersne; in 1477 William Horwood, choirmaster of Lincoln Cathedral, was appointed to teach the boys in the choir the clavichord. The oldest picture of the instrument seems to be that which figures in a manuscript compiled by Henri Arnault of Zwolle, physician to the Duke of Burgundy, in the middle of the fifteenth century, and now in the Bibliothèque Nationale in Paris.

The plan of the clavichord is as follows (see plate 1). The case is rectangular, the keyboard placed along the front. The strings, at right angles to the keys, are stretched between hitch-pins on one side and tuning pegs (wrest-pins) on the other and pass over a bridge glued to the soundboard. Unlike the harpsichord or the piano, only that part of

---

[1] The keys of the primitive organ played literally the rôle of 'keys' (Latin, *clavis*) opening a passage into the pipes for air, from which we derive our word 'keys' for the white and black notes of the piano fingerboard. To distinguish the keys of the primitive organ, the habit arose of inscribing on each the letter (from A to G) which corresponded to the respective notes. When notation by lines and staves was established, the same letters, though gradually altered in appearance, were written at the beginning of the stave to indicate the pitch position of the notes. They, too, retained the name of 'clefs' or keys – names which survive in our C, G, and F 'clefs'.

[2] This ambiguity, a result of carelessness in the language of the time, will be met with again in the various names by which the harpsichord and the piano were at one time called. The same ambiguity is found in the case of many other instruments. For instance, the names 'lyre' and 'cithara' were in the Middle Ages applied to instruments of all kinds.

16

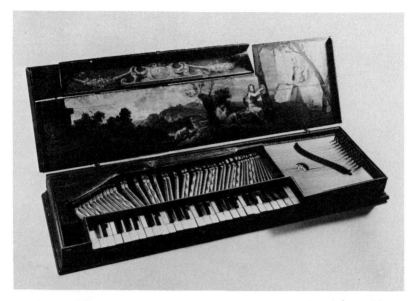

1 Clavichord by Johann Weiss, Stuttgart, 1702. Compass C – c³, but without
C♯ . Fretted. *Deutsches Museum, Munich.*

the string between the point where it is struck and the bridge is allowed
to vibrate, the remaining section of the string, namely that between the
point where it is struck and the hitch-pins, being damped by a strip of
felt. The percussion instrument, the striker, is called the 'tangent', and
consists of a small blade of metal fixed to the far end of the key. When
the key is depressed, the lever see-saws and the tangent strikes the string
from underneath (see Appendix, Figure 1). The rôle of the tangent is
not limited to originating the sound. It also determines the pitch by
limiting the vibrating part of the string, just as the finger does on the
fingerboard of a violin. The tangent must therefore continue to press
against the string instead of releasing it to vibrate freely, as does the jack
of the harpsichord or the rebounding hammer of the piano.

The first clavichords (of which not one example survives and which
we can only mentally reconstruct from contemporary drawings) had a
range of only three or three-and-a-half diatonic octaves from C. At first
only one accidental was added to the keyboard, the flattened seventh (B
flat), to be joined later by the sharpened fourth (F sharp). During the
fifteenth and sixteenth centuries the compass gradually became
chromatic. In dealing with the piano keyboard, we shall have occasion
to speak of the inconveniences which arose from this step-by-step

2   Clavichord by Gottfried Horn, Nickern, 1790. Compass FF – f³. Unfretted.
Detail of action. *Deutsches Museum, Munich.*

development of the early keyboard.

From the beginning the clavichord foreshadowed the rectangular shape of the future 'square' piano. The natural keys were usually made of boxwood and were much shorter than those of today. The case, small in size, was without legs; it was placed on a table, a chair, or simply across the knees; and it was cheap.[1]

In the beginning the clavichord had fewer strings than keys, the same string being made to produce two or even three notes. As we have just seen, the tangent not only originated the sound but also determined the pitch. Advantage was taken of this fact to obtain from a single string several notes by means of as many tangents, fixed at appropriate distances, under the same string. Here is an example of how forty-five notes were divided among twenty-six strings (the numerals indicate the strings, starting from the bass):

1, C; 2, D; 3, E; 4, F; 5, G; 6, A; 7, B flat and B natural; 8, c and c sharp; 9, d and d sharp; 10, e; 11, f and f sharp; 12, g and g sharp;

[1] 'But such clavichords', coldly observes the organist Jacob Adlung, cited by Curt Sachs, 'are good to burn when one wishes to cook fish'.

13, a; 14, b flat and b; 15, c^1 and c^1 sharp; 16, d^1 and d^1 sharp; 17, e^1; 18, f^1 and f^1 sharp; 19, g^1 and g^1 sharp; 20, a^1; 21, b^1 flat and b^1; 22, c^2 and c^2 sharp; 23, d^2, d^2 sharp and e^2; 24, f^2, f^2 sharp and g^2; 25, g^2 sharp, a^2 and b^2 flat; 26, b^2 and c^3.

Clavichords of this sort were called 'fretted' (German *gebunden*). Two notes produced by the same string could not of course be sounded simultaneously. The first 'unfretted' (*bundfrei*) clavichord is said to have been constructed in 1725 by Daniel Faber, an organist of Crailsheim. The system of tuning by equal temperament, at that time recently introduced, made it desirable that each note should have its independent string. Naturally, the unfretted instrument was bigger. But the 'fretted' clavichord continued in use until about 1750, doubtless because of its more convenient size, its greater ease of tuning and its cheaper price.

Another peculiarity of numerous clavichords, as well as many harpsichords, spinets and organs as late as the middle of the eighteenth century is even more remarkable. This is the so-called 'short octave', inherited from the primitive organ. The origin of the short octave was this: since chromatic notes were rarely utilised in the lowest register, the early organ builder took advantage of the fact to economise by omitting the corresponding pipes, which were long and expensive. The keyboard might, for instance, *appear* to end in the bass with the note E. But in reality this E gave the note C. In the same way the apparent F sharp produced the note D, the G sharp, E. The rest of the keys proceeded in the usual way. To play the ascending scale of C in the bass, the organist thus played (apparently) E, F sharp, G sharp (then slipping back) F, G, A, etc. The instrument did not become really chromatic until it reached B flat. This arrangement was extended to the clavichord. That is why certain early keyboard compositions finish with the left hand apparently spanning the tenth C – E, which, in actual execution, only represented an octave.

The short octave took still other forms, notably that in which the lowest accidental keys were transversely divided in half, each half corresponding with a string, the front half giving D and E, the back F sharp and G sharp. This device was called sometimes the 'broken octave'.

Another characteristic of the clavichord was purely technical. In the case of the piano the hammer, having struck the string, rebounds, leaving the string free to vibrate so long as the key remains depressed. In other words the sound, having once been produced, cannot be further modified. In the case of the clavichord, however, the tangent

19

remains pressed against the string until the key is released, so that the player retains control over the note he has just struck. By varying the pressure of his finger on the key he can obtain a kind of vibrato, analogous to that produced on the violin by the same method.

This tremolo, known in German as *bebung* and in French as *tremblement,* was much appreciated in Germany, where the piano was criticised later for being incapable of it. It was indicated in compositions for the clavichord by a series of dots, surmounted by a curved line; but in general its application was left to the taste of the executant (who was, however, advised not to abuse it). In his celebrated treatise *Versuch über die wahre Art das Clavier zu spielen* (1753), Carl Philipp Emanuel Bach recommends it for 'long and affectionate' notes to which it imparts a kind of insistent pathos.

By the eighteenth century the clavichord had attained its final form. It was still rectangular; the keyboard, seldom longer than five octaves, was set into the front of the case. The strings were often doubled, especially in the bass, and sometimes even trebled in an attempt to achieve greater sonority. Without as a rule rivalling the striking luxury

3 Clavichord by Barthold Fritz, Brunswick, 1751. Compass FF – a^3. Unfretted. *Victoria and Albert Museum, London.*

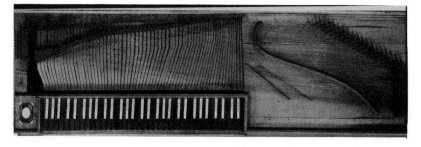

4 Interior view of the same instrument. Note the separate four-foot bridge serving the lowest twenty keys, which have two unison strings and one octave.

of many harpsichords, the instrument had taken on an elegant appearance, the interior of the lid being ornamented with paintings, the keys veneered with ivory, tortoise-shell, mother-of-pearl, etc.

The clavichord demanded a very delicate technique. Contemporaries claimed that it took something like fifteen years to master it. As the tangent when it struck the string at the same time also slightly stretched it, the slightest inequality of pressure betrayed itself in corresponding alterations of pitch. It was said that C. P E. Bach would not judge a harpsichordist without first having heard him play the clavichord.

The tone of the clavichord is agreeable, very pure (being free from the mechanical sound of the harpsichord), very expressive, and capable of considerable nuance within a limited dynamic range, but extremely weak and short-lived. For this last reason the instrument was sometimes called the 'muffled spinet' or the 'muette'. People spoke of its huskiness (*heiserkeit*). A girl who was carrying on a secret love-affair was said 'to be playing the clavichord'.

This feebleness of sound restricted the instrument to domestic use, and even in chamber music it was not really suitable for ensemble playing. The Benedictine rule of the sixteenth century authorised the construction and use of the clavichord in the cloisters.

It is worth dwelling here for an instant on the rôle played by the clavichord in the history of keyboard music, a subject until comparatively recently not sufficiently understood in Western Europe as a whole, or even in Germany. It may seem strange that Schweitzer, in his book on Bach, should ignore the clavichord, making only a passing reference to it *à propos* of a passage from Forkel's biography of 1802 which we shall discuss a little later. Schweitzer appeared not even to know the nature, far less the expressive properties, of the clavichord

21

which, for him is a 'kind of harpsichord'. In his learned little treatise on *Les Clavecinistes,* Pirro has not a word to say about the mechanism of the clavichord, although in England Arnold Dolmetsch was one of the first to champion the clavichord, and recorded several Bach Preludes and Fugues on this instrument.

Recently, however, a whole literature has grown up around it, a series of works and articles by Nef, Auerbach, Landowska, Bodky, Neupert and others. Among the most remarkable of these works is Cornelia Auerbach's *Die deutsche Clavichordkunst* (1930).[1] The author has collected so many documents pertaining to the clavichord that she may be said to have exhausted the subject. But we shall see that the question is nevertheless still obscure and full of uncertainty.

Early keyboard music was played on the organ, or the clavichord or the harpsichord, according to the taste of the executant; but more usually on the organ, which at this time is the *klavier,* the 'keyboard', *par excellence.* The organ was played in private homes, on 'portative organs', particularly in Germany. We may note, moreover, that the first composers for the clavichord in England, France and Germany, were nearly all court or church organists.

'If one can play the organ', wrote Elias Ammerbach in 1571, 'one can also play the other keyboard instruments'. This was to remain true until the middle of the eighteenth century. Henri Dumont was as renowned as a harpsichordist as he was an organist, and Bach was a master of both instruments. The celebrated contest between Handel and Scarlatti took place on the harpsichord and the organ alternately.

Today, when the practice of domestic music is restricted mainly to the piano, it is difficult for us to imagine a time when three essentially different instruments were commonly used, and when it was not unusual to find in middle-class homes several of these keyboard instruments. The indifference as to what instrument a piece was played on is expressed in the title-page instructions of the time: 'For organ, clavichord or harpsichord' – or even for any instrument at all, *ogni strumenti* 'all instruments', the choice really being limited only by the range and technical peculiarities of each individual instrument.

This latitude extended to the orchestra as well, where the parts, even with Bach, appear frequently to be interchangeable. We must wait until the Viennese School before finding musical themes inspired by the timbre and quality of the instruments themselves. Slowly, however, distinct styles, due to the properties of the instuments themselves,

[1] More recent studies include those by Boalch and Russell (see Bibliography) (Ed.)

evolved. The organ style was characterised by its sustained notes; the harpsichord style by its ornamentation. Discrimination between the organ, the clavichord and the harpsichord was established little by little. In 1636, Mersenne insisted that the instrument specified by the composer must be played. The more austere repertoire became the preserve of the organ, finally limited to the church, while the clavichord and the harpsichord continued to share the secular repertoire. But it is here that the uncertainty begins, yet again increased by the ambiguity of the term *klavier* which had passed from the organ to both clavichord and harpsichord.

The clavichord was little played in France. C. P. E. Bach emphasised the French lack of interest in the instrument. The musical dictionary of the *Encyclopédie méthodique* does not even give it a separate article; Hüllmandel only mentions it in his article on the *Harpsichord* as a 'forerunner' of the latter instrument.

In England the clavichord enjoyed a certain popularity. Henry VII's Queen, Elizabeth of York, played it; in 1502, James IV of Scotland played the clavichord to his fiancée Margaret. Soon after this, however, it gave way to the virginals and the spinet. In Italy and the Netherlands it was seldom played. In Germany, fatherland of the clavichord, this general indifference towards the instrument was advanced as an argument against it by its adversaries.

In fact, the clavichord had not suffered as badly in Germany as elsewhere from the competition of the harpsichord. Described in 1618 by Praetorius as the 'foundation of all keyboard instruments' it still remained for Walther (*i.e.* in 1732) 'the first grammar of all keyboard executants'. It was still popular because of its cheapness, its convenient size and shape and its discreet tone – for in those days no one would have dreamed of letting loose in an ordinary drawing-room the thundering chords of a grand piano.

Among the clavichord's adherents the most illustrious was Bach, whose love for the instrument is affirmed by Forkel, his first biographer (1802):

'He liked best to play upon the clavichord; the harpsichord, though certainly susceptible of a very great variety of expression, had not soul enough for him; and the piano was in his lifetime too much in its infancy and still much too coarse to satisfy him. He therefore considered the clavichord as the best instrument for study, and, in general, for private musical entertainment. He found it the most convenient for the expression of his most refined thoughts, and did not believe it possible to produce from any harpsichord or pianoforte such a variety in the gradations of tone as on this instrument, which is, indeed, poor in tone, but on a small scale extremely flexible.'

Bach's two eldest sons shared their father's preference. Wilhelm Friedemann, according to Forkel, played the clavichord 'with extraordinary delicacy', and in his sonatas 'shows that he understands all its resources'. Carl Philipp Emanuel preferred the clavichord to the piano because of its greater expressiveness.

'The more recent pianoforte, when it is sturdy and well built, has many fine qualities, although its touch must be carefully worked out, a task which is not without difficulties. It sounds well by itself and in small ensembles. Yet, I hold that a good clavichord, except for its weaker tone, shares equally in the attractiveness of the pianoforte and in addition features the vibrato and *portato* which I produce by means of added pressure after each stroke. It is at the clavichord that a keyboardist may be most exactly evaluated. A good clavichord must have in addition to a lasting, caressing tone, the proper number of keys, extending at the very least from the great octave C to the three-lined *e*. The upper limit is needed for the playing of scores written for other instruments. Composers like to venture into this high register because many instruments can reach it quite easily. The keys must be properly weighted to help raise the fingers after each stroke. In order that the strings may be attacked as well as caressed and be capable of expressing purely and clearly all degrees of forte and piano, they must be resilient. Taut strings keep the tone of a vibrato pure; yet they should not be too taut or they will sound strained and the performer will be unable to achieve any volume; on the other hand, if they are too loose, they will sound impure and unclear if they sound at all. The keys must not fall too deep, and the pegs must be tightly fitted so that the strings will be capable of withstanding the full force of an attack and remain in tune.' (*Essay on the True Art of Playing Keyboard Instruments.*)

On 12th October 1772, while staying in Hamburg, Dr Charles Burney visited C. P. E. Bach and was deeply impressed by his performance on the clavichord.

'Bach was so obliging as to sit down to his Silbermann clavichord, and favourite instrument, upon which he played three or four of his choicest and most difficult compositions, with the delicacy, precision, and spirit, for which he is justly celebrated among his countrymen. In the pathetic and slow movements, whenever he had a long note to express, he absolutely contrived to produce, from his instrument, a cry of sorrow and complaint, such as can only be effected upon the clavichord, and perhaps by himself. After dinner, which was elegantly served, and chearfully eaten, I prevailed upon him to sit down again to a clavichord, and he played, with little intermission, till near eleven o'clock at night. During this time, he grew so animated and possessed, that he not only played, but looked like one inspired. His eyes were fixed, his under lip fell, and drops of effervescence distilled from his countenance. He said, if he were to be set to work frequently, in this manner, he should grow young again.' (*The Present State of Music in Germany and the Netherlands.*)

From this time onwards the clavichord had to struggle on the one hand against the harpsichord, which had now arrived at its supreme perfection, and on the other against the piano, which was still crude and rudimentary, but also possessed of that very capacity for nuance and expression which had been the clavichord's greatest advantage over the harpsichord.

There was a considerable revival of interest in the clavichord in the second half of the eighteenth century. It was peculiarly in harmony with the romantic movement which stirred Germany at this time, that wave of sentimentalism which was a few years later to produce the literary school of *Sturm und Drang*. The clavichord, with its special capacity for expression, its subtlety of nuance, the pathos of its *bebung,* was the instrument specially designed for expressing such romantic states of the soul. In contrast, French musical taste of the time still remained firmly attached to the classical tradition incorporated in the music of the harpsichord.

However, this romantic movement did not find, to express it, one of those figures of genius who immortalise a whole period in his artistic creations. It corresponds rather to the Mannheim School, cradle of the modern symphony, midway between the older classics and the great Viennese composers. Its keyboard music is represented by a series of composers nowadays more or less forgotten: Johann Wilhelm Hässler (1747-1822), Christian Gottlob Neefe, Beethoven's first teacher (1748-1798), Johann Friedrich Reichardt (1752-1814), and Daniel Gottlob Türk (1750-1813), all of whom are overshadowed by the engaging figure of Carl Philipp Emanuel Bach.

But C. P. E. Bach himself was often an ingenious rather than an inspired innovator and his keyboard works, like those of the composers just mentioned, find little place in the musical repertoire of today. They have been rescued from oblivion only by the science of musicology which often attributes an importance to them in which documentary interest is sometimes confused with artistic value.

25

The repertoire in question is made up of intimate pieces, sentimental or even tearful, underlined by such titles as: 'Do not weep, we shall meet again' (Türk). Doubtless Schumann, had he been born a century earlier, would have written for the clavichord. Little dances, transcriptions of songs, *handstücke* (little instruction pieces), pastorales, rondos, were adapted for the instrument. In a word, the clavichord's repertoire comprised all those short and simple pieces marked by 'expressiveness' and 'affection' or *affetto* – that interior *affetto* not without sentimentality which the Germans call *gemüt*.

Simplicity to the point of poverty (but an intentional poverty) typifies this school of composers. The well-knit polyphony of J. S. Bach is quite forgotten. The Türks and the Hässlers were often content to write in two parts only, leaving an enormous void in between. Passages like the following:

are tolerable only on the clavichord, thanks to its intimacy, its capacity for portamento and vibrato, which can supply a kind of inner harmony. If we had to revive such pieces for the modern piano, it would be necessary to harmonise them properly, to add new parts, as with a figured bass. Such economy and bareness of writing would have been reason enough to condemn to oblivion this repertoire, of only moderate artistic interest, which rose ephemerally between the majestic mountain peaks of the old classics and the later Viennese School.

In the long run the same oblivion was destined to overtake the School's acknowledged instrument, the clavichord. Even so a few notable instruments were built in the late eighteenth century. We have said that the vogue of the clavichord extended alongside that of the harpsichord and that it competed with the early pianoforte. In 1760 a builder named Johann David Gerstenberg made a 'pedal-clavichord with six rows of strings, two keyboards and a pedal board'. Builders who had abandoned the harpsichord still made clavichords; Silbermann, the first important piano maker, invented a *cembal d'amour,* which was an elaborate clavichord with strings of twice the normal speaking length, struck centrally by the tangents so that each half of the string sounded the same note and transmitted the sound to its own soundboard. Adlung's *Musica mechanica organoedi* (1768) gives a detailed account of the instrument's construction, but no contemporary specimens have survived.

A sort of lingering sentimentality inspired the defenders of the clavichord. As late as 1793 the *Musikalisches Wochenblatt,* reprinting an advertisement published in Paris for Pascal Taskin's piano, added this nostalgic commentary: 'This proud instrument appears to be infinitely removed from the modest clavichord which, even if it is unable to replace an entire orchestra, remains among all other keyboard instruments the most supple and moving, with most power to affect the sentiments'. We may recall that Mozart himself (who was so cheerfully to abandon the harpsichord for the piano) still played the clavichord, the construction of which continued in Germany up to the beginning of the nineteenth century.

But then it ceased. Favourite instrument of a period and of the second-magnitude composers who represented it, the clavichord was to disappear with them before the triumphant piano. Already at the end of the eighteenth century the clavichord was no longer spoken of except with reticence. In his text book *Die wahre Art das Pianoforte zu spielen* (1797) Milchmeyer speaks of the clavichord with undisguised contempt. A few years later it was forgotten, and this oblivion was to last until the middle of the present century.

It is interesting today to see the clavichord once again making its reappearance, discreetly, in conformity with its character, a revival quite independent of the archæological preoccupations which led to the renaissance of the harpsichord, a revival among ordinary people, among the young, thanks to the same qualities which made it popular in earlier days – its intimacy and its quite democratic cheapness.

Leaving at present the history of the clavichord and its repertoire, let us go back for a moment to a question not less important, a problem at one time entirely neglected, but today of the greatest importance, not only to the arid field of the musicologist, but to the execution of the living art. The question is whether we should use the clavichord in our interpretation of the oldest classics and in particular of the keyboard music of Johann Sebastian Bach.

The popularity of the instrument in the time of Bach's predecessors makes plausible Bodky's opinion that numerous compositions of an

5 Clavichord by Johann Adolph Hass, Hamburg, 1763. Compass FF – f³.
Unfretted. Four-foot bridge serving the lowest nineteen strings, which
have two unison strings and one octave. The stand is not original. *Russell
Collection, Edinburgh.*

intimate nature by Froberger, Fischer, Pachelbel, J. C. Bach, Kuhnau
and even Haydn (though this last is more disputable) ought to be
played on the clavichord. We have noted Johann Sebastian Bach's own
sympathy with the old instrument. From this the question arises: how
much attention should we pay to this in the interpretation of his
works? On the title-pages of three of his works, the Italian Concerto,
the French Overture in B minor and the 'Goldberg' Variations, he
specified the harpsichord. Everywhere else we run into the ambiguous
term *klavier,* notably in the immortal collection of the Forty-eight
Preludes and Fugues, the *Wohltemperierte Clavier.* Thus various theories
are permissible and it is really a question of deciding for each individual
piece of music the instrument which best suits it. The pieces demanding

virtuosity and bravura should naturally be reserved for the harpsichord; the simpler, more intimate, 'singing' pieces, implying shades of expression, are better interpreted on the clavichord.

Notably among the latter are the *Noten-Büchlein* written for Anna-Magdalena and for Friedemann, the French Suites, the Little Preludes for beginners, and the Inventions. In the case of the 'Forty-eight' a discrimination might be made between the different numbers according to their differences in character. Bodky has attempted this task, admitting, however, that some are equally appropriate to the organ, the clavichord or the harpsichord. Indeed, the answer to the problem depends upon personal choice and cannot be reduced to any hard and fast rule.

Clavichord makers are difficult to list, first because the earliest 'fretted' instruments are generally unsigned; secondly because the manufacture of the instrument is often confused with that of harpsichords and pianos made in the same workshops. Among the most important clavichord makers are: Barthold Fritz (1697-1766) of Brunswick, Hieronymus Albrecht Hass (*c.* 1689-*c.* 1744) and Johann Adolph Hass (*fl.* 1740-1768), both of Hamburg, Gottfried Joseph Horn (1739-1797) and Johann Gottlob Horn (1748-1796), both of Dresden, Christian Gottlob Hubert (1714-1793) of Ansbach, Johann Paul Krämer (1743-1819) of Göttingen, Friedrich Carl Lemme (1747-1808) of Brunswick, Johann Christoff Schiedmayer (1740-*c.* 1796) of Neustadt an der Aisch, Friedrich Schmahl (*fl.* 1692) of Regensburg, Georg Friedrich Schmahl (1700-1773) of Ulm, Jakob Friedrich Schmahl (1777-1819) and Christian Carl Schmahl (1782-1815), both of Regensburg, Gottfried Silbermann (1683-1753) of Freiburg, Johann Heinrich Silbermann (1727-1799) of Strasbourg, Johann Andreas Stein (1728-1792) of Augsburg, and Johann Michael Voigt (*fl.* 1804-1812) of Schweinfurt.

The construction of the clavichord today has been taken up again, like that of the harpsichord, by innumerable makers, although the instrument's intimate nature restricts its use to the home and the recording studio.

Museums preserve a fairly large number of clavichords (though fewer than harpsichords). The oldest appears to be one dated 1543 by Domenico Pisaurensis in the Karl-Marx-Universität, Leipzig.

2 *Harpsichord, Spinet and Virginal*

A technician of genius, a Cristofori or an Erard, might, in seeking to perfect the clavichord, have hit directly upon the piano. Instead, the principle of the struck string was abandoned for that of the plucked string, only to be taken up again two hundred years later. As a result, the development of keyboard instruments made a détour for two centuries. In view of the inferiority of the harpsichord's capacity for expression compared with the clavichord, it is clear that the inventors of the new instrument were chiefly seeking for an instrument of greater sonority, one which could be heard in larger rooms and which could make itself felt in instrumental ensembles. If the clavichord is basically nothing but a dulcimer with a keyboard, the harpsichord is derived from the psaltery, an instrument itself not unlike the dulcimer, but apparently more ancient and whose strings, instead of being struck by mallets, are plucked by the fingers.

We do not know precisely when the harpsichord was invented, but it is generally believed to be about the middle of the fifteenth century (a contemporary manuscript compiled by Henri Arnault of Zwolle, physician to the Duke of Burgundy, discusses four different ways of attacking the string of the harpsichord, and there are various pictorial representations of the instrument of similar date).

The strings were no longer plucked directly by the fingers, but by a mechanical finger known as the 'jack' (Italian, *saltarello*; French, *sautereau*; German, *docke*). The jack is a small shaft of flat wood held upright at the felted far extremity of the key. It passes through a wooden mortice which keeps it vertical, and emerges from a hole in the soundboard beneath the string it is intended to pluck. The upper part of the jack is furnished with a hinged tongue which can move backwards and forwards. From this tongue a crow quill juts out. A felt damper is fixed to the rigid upper part of the jack.

When the key is depressed the jack rises, and the jutting quill plucks the string in passing. Then the jack falls back again by its own weight, and the damper stops the vibration of the string. In falling back, it is obvious that the quill must not catch against the string, for if it did the jack would remain in suspense. That is why the tongue is hinged. On the return journey the tongue falls back and the quill slips silently past the string. When the action is completed a delicate spring, made of hog's bristle, pushes the tongue back into position. A wooden bar (the jack rail) is fixed above the row of jacks to prevent their jumping out of their respective holes in the event of the keys being struck too hard (see Appendix, Figures 2 and 3).

The mechanism of this action, although complicated to describe, is really very simple, but it requires regular and careful adjustment. We can imagine the irregularities of tone which could be caused by unequal length and thickness of the quills (which were soaked in olive oil to harden them). For this reason conscientious players 'feathered' their own jacks. Bach was particularly skilful in this operation, which he could accomplish in a quarter of an hour.

From the beginning of the seventeenth century the strings were made of steel for the treble and middle range and of brass for the bass. Mersenne also mentions silver, gold and even silk[1]. As with the clavichord the strings are strung between fixed hitch-pins and tuning pegs (see plate 8). The vibrating section is no longer limited by a strip of felt, but extends between two bridges. The soundboard is three or four millimetres thick and is sometimes pierced by a sound-hole covered over by cardboard, wood, ivory or gilded lead. The keys were made first of boxwood, then of ivory and finally of bone, a material which is less

[1] The use of silk strings is common in the Far East where, in the classic instruments (the Chinese *Kin* and the Japanese *Koto*) they produce excellent results. These instruments, thanks, no doubt, to their being doped with some substance unknown to us, never got out of tune.

6 Harpsichord by Jerome of Bologna, Rome, 1521. Compass C – d³, with short octave. Two unison strings of eight-foot pitch (the second added later). The instrument, characteristically, is of cypress wood, and rests within an outer case who'se tooled and gilded leather covering is of late seventeenth-century date. The base of the instrument is cut away below the lowest fourteen keys, to permit the operation of cords or trackers, originally attached to pedals. It is the oldest surviving harpsichord whose authenticity is undisputed. *Victoria and Albert Museum, London.*

apt to turn yellow. The case and the soundboard in Italy were generally made of cypress; in Flanders, France, Germany and England usually of pine or deal.

The nomenclature of the instrument is as obscure as it is confused, the terms harpsichord, spinet and virginal being freely used, often to denote the same kind of instrument, whereas in fact it took on several distinct forms. The harpsichord proper is wing-shaped, with the strings running from a wrest-plank immediately above the keys to hitch-pins disposed along the bent side and running in the same direction as the keys themselves (see plate 8). Its smaller derivatives, the spinet and the virginal (in both of which the jack-action is the same as in the harpsichord), assumed various shapes. The earlier Italian spinets were polygonal, the Flemish and English spinets of the sixteenth and seventeenth centuries (usually called virginals in England) were rectangular, and they both differed from the harpsichord in that the strings

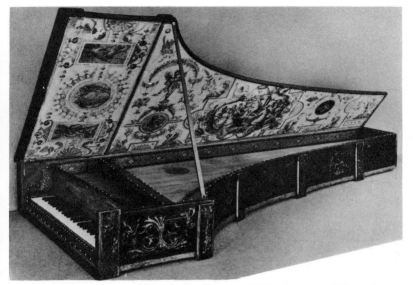

7 Harpsichord by Giovanni Baffo, Venice, 1574. Compass GG – c³, with
short octave (for alterations to the instrument's compass see Victoria and
Albert Museum Catalogue, 1968, Vol I, pp 33-5). The instrument is
mainly of cypress wood, and rests within an outer case (with later
decoration). Two unison strings of eight-foot pitch (a four-foot register
was added at some time, but was subsequently removed). *Victoria and
Albert Museum, London.*

ran across the keys, roughly at right-angles to them, from a wrest-plank
placed diagonally across the left and the back of the instrument to
hitch-pins at the right, or vice versa (see plate 18); the jacks extending
from a point in the soundboard near the front of the case at the bass
end of the keyboard to the back of the case at the treble end. The later
English, German and French spinets, of the late seventeenth century
and the eighteenth century, were really small harpsichords with the
wrest-plank placed above the keys and with the strings running to
hitch-pins disposed along the bent side at the right, but with the long
side running diagonally across the back of the instrument, at an angle
of about 45 degrees to the keyboard, with the result that the bent side
is shorter, and often more steeply curved, than in a harpsichord (see
plate 23).

   The name of the harpsichord in German is *kielflügel*; in French,
clavecin, and in Italian, *cembalo,* which is a contraction of *gravicembalo* or
clavicembalo (literally, and misleadingly, 'keyed dulcimer', for as we have

seen, it is really a 'keyed psaltery').

The word spinet (Italian, *spinetta*; German, *spinett*; French, *épinette* may derive from the fact that the instrument is plucked by a kind of spine (or in Italian *spina*). Banchieri (1565-1634) believed that it originated from the name of the Venetian Spinetus, who was supposed to have invented the spinet.

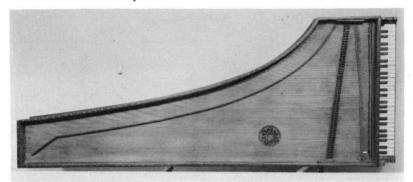

8 Interior of the instrument in plate 7, showing the 'rose' of parchment, and demonstrating the unusual length of harpsichords by Baffo and other Venetian makers – and this despite the fact that the instrument was shortened, possibly by as much as one foot, in the eighteenth century.

The smaller octave harpsichord which could be superimposed on the larger instrument, was known under such various names as the 'little spinet', the *ottavina, spinettina, spinetta da serenata* and *oktav-Spinett* (see plate 19).

As we have seen, the spinet in England became the virginal or virginals, also a name of disputed origin. One theory was that it came from the virgin Queen Elizabeth, an enthusiastic player of the virginals (see plate 18); but the word was already in use before she was born. Still other theories are that the name arose from the instrument's popularity with young ladies; again that it derived from the ancient sign, the *virga*, which somewhat vaguely resembled the shape of the jack; and finally that the thin tone-quality of the virginals recalled the *Jungfernregal* (or 'maiden' stop) of the German organ. According to Van den Borren, the name virginals designated in England in the fifteenth and sixteenth centuries every kind of plucked keyboard instrument. It is only from the seventeenth century that it was limited to small instruments. The name crossed the Channel and passed into other languages. Virdung (*Musica getutscht und ausgezogen*) used it in 1511. But the word generally refers to the rectangular instrument, while in England it was applied

9 Claviorganum by Lodewijk Theeuwes, London, 1579. Compass C – c³.
There were originally two unison strings of eight-foot pitch and one of
four, but of the action only the keyframe and one key survive; only
fragments of the organ action survive. The case of the harpsichord (and
of the organ) is of oak, the soundboard of pine. The harpsichord itself is
the earliest known one to have been made in England (though Theeuwes
originally came from Antwerp). *Victoria and Albert Museum, London.*

indifferently to those of any shape.

The earliest harpsichords (of which the instrument made in 1521 by
Jerome of Bologna in Rome, in the Victoria and Albert Museum,
London (plate 6), is a characteristic example) had a compass of about
four octaves and one, or occasionally two strings to each note. However,
from an early stage attempts were made to enrich the harpsichord by the
multiplication of strings and, in consequence, of the rows of jacks.
While the Italians coupled two strings in unison, the Antwerp builders
added a third string tuned an octave higher. The range of the keyboard
increased only gradually with the gradual increase in range of the music
composed for it.

Attempts were also soon made to enrich the instrument by adding
diversity to the quality of the sounds it could produce, as with the stops

10   Harpsichord by Hans Ruckers the Elder, Antwerp, 1590. Compass FF – f³
(originally GG – c³), with short octave. Two unison strings of eight-foot
pitch and one of four, operated by four rows of jacks (upper keyboard:
eight-foot quill; lower keyboard: four-foot quill, eight-foot quill, eight-
foot leather). This is one of the earliest instruments by a member of the
famous Ruckers family, although it was radically rebuilt (*'mis à
ravalement'*) in Paris during the eighteenth century, probably by François
Blanchet or Pascal Taskin; the characteristic block-printed paper decoration
of the Ruckers has, however, been retained on the frontboard and on the
cheeks. *Conservatoire National de Musique, Paris.*

on an organ. Experiments were made with the point at which the quill attacked the string. This striking-point is of great importance[1]. If the string is plucked near the nut a pungent, incisive tone results (this quality was exploited particularly in the 'lute stop', which is described below); if farther from it (as in the earlier polygonal and rectangular spinets) the tone is rounder and fuller.

Another variety was obtained by using different materials for the plectra in the jacks: the classic substance was crow quill, but whalebone, shell, horse hoof, brass and even wood were tried, yet the supremacy of quill was not seriously challenged until the introduction of buff leather plectra in the 1760s (see page 38).

Other attempts to vary the tone included several different kinds of stop, the most important of which were the 'buff' or 'harp' stop (often misleadingly referred to as the 'lute' stop), and the lute stop proper. The buff stop consisted of a series of small pads of buff leather or felt which could be slid against the strings at a point adjacent to the nut, thereby partially muting them and producing a harp-like pizzicato effect. The lute stop, a constructionally much more complicated device, involved a special row of jacks plucking the strings at a point a short distance beyond the nut which produced a tone of distinctive, nasal quality (such as can be obtained on the lute when the strings are plucked close to the bridge). Because of the extra work it necessitated the lute stop is only found on the more elaborate and sophisticated harpsichords; it was a feature often used by English makers of the later eighteenth century, notably Schudi and Kirckman.

This diversity of stops led to the doubling of the keyboard, one of the chief distinguishing marks between the harpsichord and the spinet. Doubtless the adoption of the second keyboard originated from the habit of placing the little octave spinet on top of the larger one. Prætorius observes that one can add an octave spinet to a big spinet as 'one can add turrets to towers'. A harpsichord of 1610 by Hans Ruckers in the Musée du Conservatoire in Brussels has two cases superimposed in this way, the top case half as long as the bottom, the upper keyboard exactly above the lower, but coupled with it.

The spinet, having in its doubled form given birth to the harpsichord, was not, however, abandoned. Less expensive and cumbersome than the harpsichord, it continued side by side with the clavichord to be popular as a domestic instrument.

[1] A string vibrates not only over the whole of its length, which determines the 'fundamental' or pitch of the note, but also sets up secondary, shorter vibrations. These form the harmonics or overtones which, blended with the fundamental, give the resulting sound its quality. A secondary vibration would naturally be eliminated if the quill plucked the string in the place where it arose; a harmonic would thus be lacking and the tone quality would be different.

The 'stops' were for a long time only a prolongation through the right side of the case of the wooden slides which held the jacks. They had only to be pulled out or pushed in again. Later they were more conveniently worked by way of levers ending in knobs ranged above the keyboard, like those of an organ. In modern harpsichords they are often replaced by foot pedals.

A harpsichord (for many years thought to have been owned by Bach) in the Berlin Museum offers an example of sobriety and quiet good taste. Unfortunately, it is neither signed nor dated. Constructed of pine, with no other ornamentation except the inlay work over the keyboard, it has a range of five octaves from FF (the F of the sixteen-foot organ pipe), two keyboards which could be coupled together and five 'stops' of which two act on the lower manual, two on the upper, while the fifth is a buff stop. The black and white keys are reversed.

In the eighteenth century the range of the older keyboards became insufficient and the instruments underwent numerous transformations. 'The Flemish harpsichords are so small', wrote the *Encyclopédie* in 1785, 'that the sonatas of today cannot be played on them'. The cases were lengthened and the keyboards extended. This operation was known in France as *'mettre à ravalement'*. In this way older instruments were rebuilt with as many as five octaves, 183 strings and 61 keys. Often little remained of the original instruments except the soundboard.

A double-manual harpsichord by Hans Ruckers in the Musée du Conservatoire in Brussels, undated, but certainly not older than the first quarter of the seventeenth century, gives us a characteristic example of such refurbishing. It is nine feet five inches long, but it is easy to see that it was originally shorter, an octave having been added to the bass. In adding this to the resources of the original instrument, a series of varied effects had been obtained. The total range is four octaves (the first a 'short octave') and a sixth, divided between four rows of strings. The instrument has four stops or registers, including a buff stop. (See also plate 10 which shows an earlier Ruckers harpsichord.)

Returning to the experiments with improved jacks and the different registers, we should like to make special mention of the invention of the Walloon builder, Pascal Taskin, the harpsichord *'à buffle'*. Born at Theux in 1723, Taskin emigrated at an early age to Paris where he entered the workshop of the builder François-Etienne Blanchet, whose widow he later married and to whose business he later succeeded.

In 1768 (the same year that Erard arrived in Paris) he created his harpsichord *à buffle* and from then on his reputation spread rapidly. In

1775-6 he had been the last Treasurer of the ancient corporation of Instrument Makers (the word Manufacturers was not yet used) suppressed in this last year. In 1791 he was tuner in the *Ecole royale de chant*, cradle of the present Conservatoire, and from 1781 to 1790, Keeper of the King's Instruments. The King also offered him the title of Maker of Instruments to the Court, but Taskin declined the offer and had named in his place his nephew Pascal-Joseph (1750-1829)[1]. In 1788 he presented before the Academy a new pianoforte which will be mentioned later, and two years afterwards he constructed a harp-psaltery called the 'Armandine'. He died in 1795.

In the jacks of the harpsichord à *buffle*, the crow quill is replaced by leather which gives a tone sweeter than the sharp dry twang of the quill.[2] Wanda Landowska in her book *La Musique ancienne* (1909), describes the sound as a 'caress'. The new timbre, however, was less loud than the old and not so fitted for playing with the orchestra. As well as the leathered jacks Taskin retained two rows of ordinary quilled jacks, controlled by two iron rods which, by way of a system of levers, emerged at the player's knees as 'knee pedals'. He hoped to give the harpsichord the power of graduated nuance, so ardently desired at that time, as we shall see when we come to the pianoforte.

We may say at once that in spite of the admiration, perhaps a little forced, which these innovations excited (the art of advertisement was not unknown to the Walloon builder), Taskin's knee-pedals and foot-pedals were not outstandingly successful. As far as nuance was concerned, the system could only give mediocre results, for the principle behind the harpsichord itself was at fault.

But the success of the *buffle* was immense. Taskin, 'unique inheritor of the genius of the Ruckers', according to Grétry, enjoyed one of those immediate celebrities which occur in Paris alone.[3] In every harpsichord the *buffle* replaced the quill. At this moment the harpsichords of the

---

[1] The second son of Pascal-Joseph, Henri-Joseph (1779-1852), musical page to Louis XVI, and a pupil of his aunt, Madame Couperin, composed much music, including three operas. The eminent baritone, Alexandre Taskin (1853-97), was a nephew of Henri-Joseph.

[2] The name *buffle* referred to the Italian ox and meant originally oxhide or buff-leather. By extension it was used to describe any leather which had been treated with olive oil to harden it.

[3] One should read on this subject the very long *Letter on the Harpsichord en peau de buffle, invented by Monsieur Pascal Taskin,* addressed in 1773 to the *Journal de musique* by the Abbé Trouflant, Canon of Nevers, 'great musician, organist of his Church and one of the ablest theoreticians of the century', according to La Borde, who reproduces the letter in his *Essays.* It was also reproduced in the *Encyclopédie*, and finally as a separate booklet. We quote a few lines of this letter, a characteristic example of the warmth and enthusiasm with which churchmen (such as the Abbé Arnaud with Gluck and Father Kircher with Carissimi) used to extol the artists they championed. 'Never before has anyone succeeded in the task of graduating sound, as nature and the taste of a delicate ear and

Ruckers and of Couchet were still in favour in France, but even they had to be 'redecorated' and above all fitted à buffle. Taskin (now become 'Master Pascal') was just the man for these transformations, and thus, ironically, he had hardly any time left in which to build instruments himself.[1]

In the *Placards, Announcements and Diverse Notices* for the years 1752 to 1790, E. de Bricqueville (in his book *Les ventes d'instruments de musique*) found the name Ruckers forty-nine times and Taskin not once. Today examples of Taskin's work are extremely rare. The pianist Jacques Herz had a two-manual harpsichord by Taskin, which, at his death (1880), is believed to have gone to America. The baritone Taskin had two, one of which came into the possession of the pianist Diémer. The Belle Skinner collection of instruments at Holyoke, Mass., contains a charming spinet by Taskin dated 1778, which is said to have graced the boudoir of Marie-Antoinette at the Trianon. Only two Taskin harpsichords are to be found in public collections: one of 1769 (with quill on the upper manual and leather on the lower) in the Russell Collection in Edinburgh (see plate 15), and one of 1786 (quilled throughout) in the Victoria and Albert Museum in London.[2]

The success of the *buffle* crossed the frontiers of France, and has lasted until our day. In Germany the celebrated Abbé Vogler (the builder of a particularly ingenious 'simplified' organ, and the first teacher of Weber and Meyerbeer), found in the lower register of the *buffle* 'an unknown splendour', the 'tone of a bass-viol'. J. C. Oesterlin, in Berlin, employed the *buffle* after 1773. It is frequently found in modern harpsichords.

A question arises at this point which we confess ourselves unable to answer. How far does Taskin's famous invention really belong to him? The knee-pedals were not themselves a novelty. In 1676 John Hayward

---

a sensitive soul demand. . . . It was reserved to Monsieur Pascal Taskin to triumph over the obstacles which had been too much for his predecessors. After deep meditation, this artist, as ingenious as he is modest, determined to try every sort of material in order to draw forth the sweetest sounds' (here follows a detailed analysis of the new mechanism). 'What prodigious variety in an instrument previously so intractable! The magic of the sounds which it makes today captivates the ear of the listener, charms his heart, enchants and ravishes him . . . The pleasure which you will enjoy when you listen to this instrument will soon engender another pleasure, not less delightful to the gently nurtured, that of gratitude'.

[1] A harpsichord by Taskin dated 1770 was found at the Menus in Paris; Madame du Barry had one at Versailles for which she paid three thousand livres, the builder delivered one dated 1774 to the Farmer-General Laborde, another to Madame d'Hibbert.
[2] Only one other Taskin harpsichord is known to be in existence in a private collection in Paris. (Ed.)

11   Harpsichord by Jean Couchet, Antwerp, *c* 1650. Compass FF – c³. Two strings of eight-foot pitch, and one of four, operated by four rows of jacks (upper keyboard: eight-foot leather, lute; lower keyboard: two eight-foot leather, four-foot leather). The stops are attached directly to the jack slides, and protrude from the right-hand side of the case. The jackrail for the lute stop can be seen in front of the main jackrail, and at a slight angle to it. *Metropolitan Museum of Art, New York* (The Crosby Brown Collection of Musical Instruments, 1889).

had constructed in London a harpsichord in which the volume could be graduated and the tone modified by means of four pedals. Kirckman used pedals at least from 1761. In France the Académie des Sciences had awarded a certificate of praise to a Grenoble builder, named Berger, for a mechanism 'which gave the spinet the *crescendo*; the knee or the foot presses a lever, causing the sound to be louder or softer'. Details of the mechanism are unfortunately lost.

But the *buffle* itself? Taskin is said to have been told by Balbastre, court organist, that the *buffle* had been used ten years previously by the builder, Robert Richard. A viol maker called de Laine, in the *Avant-coureur* of 1771, claimed the invention as his own. A passage in the *Encyclopédie* of 1785 mentions harpsichords 'which instead of quills have jacks mounted with pieces of leather, somewhat in the same way as those made today by Monsieur de Laine and Monsieur Pascal Taskin'. It thus seems that harpsichords of an earlier period had already employed the *buffle* principle. From this many authorities have concluded that the invention was earlier than Pascal Taskin.[1]

But this contention is not easily substantiated, for several reasons. In the first place, the most reliable older authorities (Virdung, Praetorius, Mersenne, Kircher) only mention the quill, never leather. The same is true in the rules for harpsichord building and testing of the Antwerp Guild of St Luke. In Taskin's own time the *Encyclopédie* (in the article *Art of the Instrument Maker*) speaks only of crow quills, the *buffle* being reserved for a separate chapter which has the significant title 'Harpsichords in oxhide, invented by Monsieur Pascal Taskin'.

The leather-tipped jacks which we have noted in many instruments earlier than Taskin's period, could be, in our opinion, the result of those 'redecorations' we have already spoken of. Finally, if Taskin had merely applied a process already known, how do we explain the very real sensation which the appearance of the harpsichord à *buffle* created?[2]

Throughout its career the harpsichord had all the while been improving and in the second half of the eighteenth century (at the moment, in fact, when it was about to disappear) it had attained great refinement. One has only to read the many columns, to study the many engraved plates that the *Art of the Instrument Maker* in the late eighteenth-century editions of the *Encyclopédie* devotes to the construction of the harpsichord's diverse parts, from the tuning pins to the case, to realise the importance and the specialisation of the industry. It foreshadowed the later importance of piano manufacture. Even the

[1] Notably de Wit (*für Instrumentenbau*) *Zeitschr.* Hipkins, in *Grove's Dictionary,* who even suggests that leather may have preceded quills, and Engel's *Descriptive Catalogue of the Musical Instruments in the Victoria & Albert Museum.*

[2] Russell (*The Harpsichord and Clavichord*), however, describes an unrestored harpsichord by Kirckman dated 1768 which was equipped with leather plectra, which proves that the practice was not unknown in England at least, before Taskin's 'invention'. (Ed.)

thickness of the strings is carefully considered, and for fifty-nine strings fourteen different gauges are specified, one gauge of the thicker brass strings serving two, three or four notes, and one gauge of the thinner steel strings from four to nine. Adjustable music desks, with candle stands, were provided, as in the case of grand pianos – and indeed the later English harpsichords, with their sober, undecorated casework, already anticipate the appearance of the piano.

A curious variant of the harpsichord is the clavicytherium or upright harpsichord (Italian, *cembalo verticale*), an ancestor of our upright piano, already mentioned in the beginning of the seventeenth century. Its strings were sometimes made of gut. But this instrument was not common, probably for the same reason that at first impeded the construction of the upright piano: that is the constructional difficulties resulting from a vertical mechanism. For example, the jacks, being horizontal, could not fall back of their own weight, but had to be pushed back by a spring.

The outer appearance of the harpsichord is worth dwelling on. Old instruments were not standardised in design, as are modern pianos. The builder worked according to the taste and the purse of his client. For this reason we do not find any two instruments exactly alike. More than the clavichord, the spinet and the harpsichord were generally de luxe instruments, decorated with gilding, sculpture and veneer, inlaid with shell, mother-of-pearl, ivory, etc. A spinet by Annibale Rossi of Milan (1577), now in the Victoria & Albert Museum, London, is ornamented with some two thousand precious stones of various kinds.

But the commonest form of decoration was painting, principally on the underside of the lid. These paintings were frequently by famous artists: Brueghel, Rubens, Van Dyck, Teniers, Salvator Rosa, Boucher, all decorated harpsichords.[1]

The Antwerp builders of the sixteenth and seventeenth centuries were attached to the Guild of St Luke, which was the Guild of painters, sculptors and decorators. Apart from the normal paintings and inlay work, the instruments made in Antwerp may be distinguished from all others in other ways as well. While the Italian makers left the sound-board unpainted, their Flemish counterparts strewed it with flowers,

---

[1] It is to such works of art that we owe the destruction of many instruments, or at least the replacement of many lids. Lids are made up of two parts, one rectangular covering the keyboard, and one triangular covering the soundboard. The original triangular part, saved by its asymmetry, is still found in many old instruments, while the rectangular part has been replaced by a modern copy of an old painting. Van der Straeten stated that of twenty seventeenth-century instruments he had examined at least eighteen had been disfigured in this way.

fruit, birds and insects, framed in blue scrolls. The maker's name or his trademark was inscribed on the jack rail, on the board above the keys, or in the form of a monogram in the rose cut into the soundboard. Antwerp virginals were also remarkable for the pressed, block-printed paper decoration, with friezes in the characteristic designs of the time such as are found in the pictures of Vermeer. Pious texts or philosophical tags, sometimes of great charm, completed the ornamentation.[1] As with the bells of the period the instrument maker would frequently sign his work in some such way as *Andreas Ruckers me fecit Antwerpiae mille sexenti* (Andreas Ruckers made me at Antwerp in sixteen-hundred). The price varied greatly with the ornamentation. The sound of the harpsichord was, as we know, radically different from that of the piano. It lacked the power of nuance, of crescendo and decrescendo. It could produce different timbres and different degrees of volume, but it could not manage gradations of tone as the clavichord could. On the other hand, the silvery tone of the harpsichord had a clarity which is lacking in the grand piano of today. Its variety of timbre was developed to the extreme limit by the artifice of pedals and stops which permitted the different parts in a complex fugal composition to be clearly isolated.

The technique of playing the harpsichord is also quite different. Because it is incapable of nuance, the 'attack' of fingers on keys is virtually immaterial; the important thing is clean and precise articulation. When they first played the new piano, the last of the harpsichordists for a long while retained their old technique. Beethoven, hearing Mozart, said to Czerny that Mozart had a jerky touch, without legato, the touch of a harpsichordist.[2]

---

[1] The following are examples: *Gloria Dei - Omnes spiritus laudet Dominum - Laudate eum in cordis et organo - Musica donum Dei - Musica lætitiæ comes, medicina dolorum* (Music, companion of joy, the cure for sadness) - *Acta virum probant - Intonuit nunquam melius quod Tartara flexit, quod Delphin grata pondere vexit opus* (The instrument which melted Tartarus and which the dolphin carried never sounded more sweetly - an allusion to the citharist Arion, thrown into the sea by his companions and rescued by a dolphin) - *Concordia res parvæ crescunt, discordia maxima dilabuntur* (Harmony enlarges little things, discord destroys great) - *Musica magnorum est solamen dulce laborum* (Music is the solace of labour) - *Zijt vroolijk in den Heer, Met orgel en met snæren, En laat me, tot Gods eer, Uw stemmen sæmen pæren* (Rejoice in the Lord, On the organ and with strings, And unite your voice with mine to sing the glory of God).

Certain texts emphasise the charming appearance of the old instruments: *Tali strumenti dilettano molto alle orecchi, ancora all'occhio* (Such instruments delight the ear and the eye also) - *Rendo lieti in un tempo gli occhi ed il core* (I make joyous both the eyes and the heart).

[2] Yet we know that Mozart had very strong views about legato passages which, he said, 'should flow like oil'. An element of professional jealousy may possibly have influenced Beethoven's judgement; Mozart himself was even less complimentary about Clementi's undoubtedly highly skilled playing. (Ed.)

44

Harpsichord technique had evolved of its own accord. In the beginning, only the simpler scales being employed; the black keys were little used. As we can see in the pictures of old masters like Jan Steen and Dirk Hals, the instrumentalist kept his fingers flatter and his wrist lower than he does today. Playing with the finger-tips with hands nearly vertical, as depicted on the cover of the famous English collection of virginal music, *Parthenia*, and by certain Italian Renaissance painters, less realistic than the Dutch, can probably be dismissed as stylised.

Harpsichord fingering was completely different from modern piano fingering. The middle fingers were used almost exclusively, the thumb and little finger being forbidden. In fact, until about a century ago, piano teachers still forbade the use of the thumb for the black keys for the sake of elegance. The thumb and little finger did not, therefore, have to touch the keyboard. This rule held especially for the right hand, the left hand being sometimes allowed more licence. As an example of fingering, the following is taken from Elias Ammerbach's *Orgel oder Instrument Tablatur* (1571). It covers C to D an octave higher, and its return:

```
        C              D              C
Right hand: 2-3-2-3-2-3-2-3-4-3-2-3-2-3-2-3-2
Left hand:  4-3-2-1-4-3-2-1-2-3-2-3-2-3-2-3-4
```

In an organ piece published in Paris a century later by Nivers, a pupil of Chambonnières, the following fingering is given for a phrase ascending from A to G:

```
        A              G
Right hand: 2-3-4-3-4-3-4
Left hand:  3-2-1-2-1-2-1
```

During the eighteenth century, however, technique had necessarily advanced, as the difficulties encountered in the compositions of Bach and Scarlatti imply. The first exponent of the modern technique was C. P. E. Bach in his treatise, *Versuch über die wahre Art das Clavier zu spielen.*

We have already discussed the question whether certain of J. S. Bach's works are not best interpreted on the clavichord. The same problem exists in connection with the harpsichord. Until thirty or so years ago the point would not have arisen, the harpsichord being then as forgotten as the clavichord is now. But today the question comes up with the return to favour of the older instruments, and it has started endless controversy. The answer depends on whether an authentic or an artistic rendering is desired. An authentic interpretation of those old masters who wrote for the harpsichord before the invention of the piano naturally implies the use of the former instrument. The clean-cut contrasts of timbre and dynamics are unobtainable on the piano where they blur and shade off in the nuance of piano tone. The coupling of octaves on the piano obtained on the harpsichord by means of mechanical stops, demands octave playing which in certain older compositions is inconvenient, or even impossible.

But the music itself and the art of interpretation have the property of adapting themselves throughout the centuries. We have the right, in rendering the old classics, to interpret them for the taste of today. Indeed, in a sense, we cannot do otherwise, the interpreter not having only the right, but not being able to abstain from amalgamating (and sometimes, unfortunately, superimposing) his own personality with that of the composer. The *Chromatic Fantasia*, played on the harpsichord by Wanda Landowska in the purest traditions of Bach's time, is a perfect work of art. The same piece played by Edwin Fischer on the piano becomes a dramatic poem as deeply moving as a Beethoven sonata. It is pointless to speculate, as is sometimes done, what Bach would think of it. If he were living today he would not be the Cantor of St Thomas's, but a man thinking and feeling like ourselves – and in consequence would not have written the *Chromatic Fantasia.*

The old harpsichord players, professionals and amateurs, tuned their own instruments – not always, perhaps, with perfect accuracy. (Hence the boxes, covered by a lid, which we sometimes find incorporated in old instruments, and which were used to contain the tuning key, spare strings, etc.) The professional tuner did not appear until the end of the eighteenth century when the piano had come into general use. We will return to modern tuning when we discuss the piano.

Complicated though it is we must here go into the system of tuning the harpsichord and its predecessors, since it was this tuning which inspired Bach to write the famous *Fantasia* just mentioned, and since it is also applied to the modern piano, and indeed to all our musical practice.

The sounds of different pitch which the phenomenon of vibration puts at our disposal are infinitely more numerous than those we actually make use of.[1] Music, as distinct from mere noise, results precisely from the use of sounds which have a systematic relationship with each other, but the systems have varied from primitive times to our own day.

[1] Play, for instance, the A above middle C on the piano and its octave. The first sound results from a frequency of 440 cycles per second. As the octave of a note is always twice the note's frequency, the upper A has a cycle of 880 per second. Since each cycle varies the pitch of the note we can say that this particular octave consists of at least 440 different sounds.

Since the time of the ancient Greeks, who probably borrowed the system from Egypt, European music has been limited to the seven notes of the·octave (the *gamme heptaphone*). Alterations of half and quarter tones (chromatic and enharmonic alterations) were added only as 'accidental' colourations (*chroma* means colour). Christian liturgical chant, from which modern music sprang, while actually practising these alterations, excluded them in theory. Thus the keyboard of the primitive organ had only the seven diatonic keys. But as chromatic alterations multiplied (particularly in secular music), they found their admission both into organ-building and into theory; between the diatonic keys the 'black' notes made their appearance like outsiders, crowded in at the last moment.[1]

Nor did the admission of 'accidentals' stop there. The human voice (like members of the violin family) being capable of the subtlest gradation of pitch, the Italian madrigalists in the middle of the sixteenth century distinguished in their compositions between such notes as D sharp and E flat, G sharp and A flat. Here purely acoustical speculations were combined with humanist ideas, that is to say the preoccupation with restoring Greek musical theory with its three types of notes: diatonic, chromatic and enharmonic (division by quarter tones).

Attempts were made to adapt the harpsichord to these subtleties: a quarter-tone harpsichord was constructed in Rome about 1550 by Nicola Vicentino, and others followed. These were scarcely more than the fantasies of archæologists and acousticians. But even with ordinary spinets and harpsichords, some musicians wished to provide for quarter tones by dividing the black key D sharp/E flat, and the black key G sharp/A flat transversely into two parts in order to produce each of these four notes. In 1782 Jacques Germain, a Paris harpsichord-builder, was still making instruments of this sort. However, the usual division of the scale into twelve notes remained general.

But the important problem was to fix the exact pitch-relation between these twelve notes: in a word, to tune the instruments. A complete explanation of this process would entail mathematical details which would tire the reader. We shall confine ourselves to a résumé. We must remember in the first place that no musical sound is ever

---

[1] The abnormal arrangement of our keyboard still betrays its ancestry. All notes being nowadays of exactly the same importance, there is no reason why the keys producing five of them should be relegated to the background.

47

'pure' or isolated, but is accompanied by a whole series of less audible sounds called 'harmonics', the presence or absence or relative predominance of which constitutes the 'timbre' or colour of the sound. Harmonics occur in the following order:

and so on, in intervals closer and closer together. Starting from any note the relative intervals remain the same. Certain harmonics may be lacking, others may be reinforced; these differences condition the timbre. The order of the intervals never varies. The numerals in the above sketch also indicate the relative number of air vibrations which produce the harmonics.[1] Every time that the fundamental note executes one vibration its octave (1/2) executes two vibrations, its fifth (2/3) executes three, its fourth (3/4) four, and so on.

Our system of Western music results from scales built up on twelve fifths: C to G, G to D, etc., finally ending with B sharp, the seven octaves necessary for this process being for convenience reduced to one. But the final note in the series, namely B sharp, must become the first, that is C natural. This is where the difficulty lies. In tuning these notes rigorously by exact fifths, called Pythagorean Fifths (following the system formulated five hundred years before the Christian era by the physicist and philosopher whose name they bear) we arrive at our final note (B sharp) only to find it very slightly *higher* than our original C. The difference is called a *comma*, and is a ninth of a tone or the fifty-sixth part of an octave. From this discrepancy arises the necessity of diminishing or 'tempering' the intervals in question.

For the sake of clarity we must go back to the origins of the tuning of stringed keyboard instruments. We have seen that primitive clavichords possessed only the diatonic scale of C, into which were incorporated at first only the two 'black' notes B flat and F sharp. Tuning was done by giving four *commas* to the diatonic semitones (E-F and B-C) and five *commas* to the chromatic semitones (F-F sharp and B flat-B natural). Once the entire keyboard had become chromatic the whole tones were given their exact value of nine *commas*, divided into two equal semitones, which thus consisted of four and a half *commas*

[1] This connection is noticeable in the relative lengths of strings and organ-pipes. A string or a pipe which is half, a third, or a quarter the length of another, will give the intervals of an octave, a fifth or a fourth respectively, with the longer string, or pipe. Obviously this is a natural phenomenon and quite independent of any musical system. Thus the eleventh harmonic, dividing the interval 10/12 is actually too high for F natural and too low for F sharp. This discordance is very noticeable in the hunting horn, which is rich in the eleventh harmonic, and gives it its very special tone.

each, although the natural diatonic semitone only consisted of four. This system, known as 'unequal temperament', was only suitable for the simplest scales and for pieces which modulated little. That is why the immense majority of keyboard compositions by old composers such as Couperin and Rameau only rarely depart from the key in which they begin, and avoid modulating into remote keys. Composition, however, could not remain thus shackled. The more and more frequent use of remote keys, the gradual chromaticisation of music and bolder use of modulation demanded that all intervals should be standardised. The same demand came from organ builders, for the lateral openings in organ pipes could not be multiplied without great inconvenience. It was thus that in 1691, Andreas Werckmeister, followed in 1706 by J. J. Neidhart and afterwards by still others, formulated the system of absolute equalisation between the twelve semitones, consisting of about 4.42 *commas* each. In this system, C sharp is identical with D flat, D sharp with E flat, and so on.

Tuning by perfect fifths was abolished at a stroke. We have seen that the interval of the fifth may be represented by the fraction $2/3$, or, let us say $1.00/1.50$. Now the connection between the fundamental and its fifth in the new system of tuning is represented by the fraction $1.00000/1.49831$. The difference between these two fractions is so small that the 'tempered' fifth is for practical purposes acceptable to the ear, 'that most complaisant of organs', as Gevaert calls it.[1]

Equal temperament was fairly quickly adopted in Germany in compositions requiring the new principle by which every key could be freely used. The first of such compositions were the Enharmonic Sonatas of Christian Petzold (1677-1733) and were followed by J. S. Bach in his first collection of Twenty-four Preludes and Fugues (1722) to which he added twenty-two years later a second collection, similar to the first, the whole comprising the famous 'Forty-eight', the *Well-tempered Clavier*[2]. C. P. E. Bach also adopted equal temperament, which led him to modify the traditional keyboard fingering.

In England, which was the cradle of keyboard music, the adoption of the new system must have been easier, since the principle of it was

---

[1] It is interesting to note that the Chinese musical system, limited to five notes, or in other words, to four fifths, does not necessitate the artifice of equal temperament. Chinese singing, based on perfect fifths, is clearly distinguishable by European ears and produces at first an impression of being out of tune, when in fact it is perfectly *in* tune.

[2] We may remark in passing that the sub-title of the 'Forty-eight', 'in every major and minor key' (not incidentally, given by Bach), is not strictly correct. As well as omitting exceptional keys, such as D sharp major and A sharp, etc., he neglected the flattened keys of D, C and G, currently employed.

not unknown. The old virginalists, like John Bull (1563-1628), employed notes like E flat and D sharp, B flat and A sharp. It has been concluded from this that they must have tuned their instruments by a kind of equal temperament so that a mean should be struck between such neighbouring notes.

In France, on the other hand, and in spite of the adoption of the new system by François Couperin, equal temperament spread only slowly. Rameau, creator of the science of harmony, remained for a long while opposed to it. So did the 'Encyclopédistes'. The most resolute adversary of the new tuning was J. B. de La Borde, who, in his excellent *Essai sur la musique* (1780), rose with vehemence against 'that which is basically nothing but a mechanical trick, a kind of industry, for remedying the defects of instruments which their makers do not wish to supply with all the necessary notes and keys'.

It is amusing to read the complicated artifices invented successively by Mersenne, by Rameau and by the Encyclopédistes to avoid the disadvantages of equal temperament. Framery recommended the adoption by the harpsichord of pedals like those on a harp, which he claimed would produce the necessary alterations. De La Borde suggested a complicated system of twenty-one keys per octave, the chromatic keys divided transversely into two parts giving respectively C sharp and D flat, D sharp and E flat, etc. (Harpsichords of this sort were used in Italy under the name of *cembali spezzati* or 'broken harpsichords'.) Chiquelier, Pascal Taskin's predecessor as Keeper of the King's Instruments, was said to have constructed a harpsichord tuned in this way, but in which the twenty-one notes were supposed to be combined with equal temperament. Hüllmandel, like his colleagues of the *Encyclopédie* an enemy of equal temperament, took fright at these complications. Equal temperament, though an obvious makeshift, was at least better than all these confused speculations.

The question of tuning is intimately bound up with that of pitch, the history of which is no less lively. The idea of an 'absolute' pitch of sound was for a long time not thought of. Consequently there was great variation of pitch in the tuning of instruments, which lasted until the middle of the nineteenth century, a situation further complicated by the fact that two different pitches were recognised and practised, one for voices (originating in the Church) and another for instruments.

In Germany, at the beginning of the seventeenth century, *chorton* or 'choir' pitch was a tone lower than *kammerton* or 'chamber' pitch. Then choir pitch was raised little by little, until, about 1750, it was three semitones higher than chamber pitch. The two pitches continued to

12 Harpsichord by Thomas Hitchcock, London, *c* 1725. Compass GG – g³.
Two strings of eight-foot pitch, and one of four, operated by four rows of
jacks (upper keyboard: eight-foot, lute; lower keyboard: two eight-foot,
four-foot). The case is of walnut. The Hitchcocks were a family of
spinet-makers, many of whose instruments survive, but this is one of only
two surviving harpsichords by them. *Victoria and Albert Museum, London.*

vacillate until the final disappearance of choir pitch. But the idea of an
'absolute' pitch being still unknown, there was no firm foundation for
tuning.

The French mathematical genius Sauveur (1653-1716) had recommended as a standard the figure of 100 'vibrations' (*i.e.* 200 cycles) per
second, but this innovation did not meet with unanimous acceptance.
The variations continued until finally in 1859 an international congress
in Paris fixed treble A (the A of the one-foot organ pipe) at 435 cycles
per second. Today the pitch most commonly regarded as standard is
New Philharmonic, in which A is 440 c.p.s.

Among musical instruments the harpsichord has had one of the
longest and most glorious careers, extending over more than two
centuries. The instrument was played in middle-class homes, at royal

51

13 Interior view of the same instrument. Notice the diagonal graining of the soundboard, and the elegant curve of the tail – an unusual feature for an English harpsichord. The elaborate keys – ivory naturals with arcaded fronts, ebony accidentals with a strip of ivory inlaid – are a characteristic Hitchcock feature.

courts, in churches, in concert halls and in the theatre. Marie of Burgundy, Eleanor and Margaret of Austria, Mary Stuart and Queen Elizabeth played the spinet; Louis XIV had his harpsichord professors. The organist and harpsichordist Louis Marchand (1669-1732), one of the most highly esteemed masters in Paris, charged a louis d'or for lessons. Poems were written to the harpsichord which La Fontaine said he preferred to the opera:

'De cette aimable enfant le clavecin unique
Me touche plus qu'*Isis* et toute sa musique'.[1]

The greatest masters of music composed for the harpsichord, inspired both by its technical advantages and by its limitations; in Spain, Cabezón and D. Scarlatti; in England, Byrd, Bull, Purcell and Handel; in Italy, the Gabrielis, Merulo, Frescobaldi and Pasquini; in the Netherlands, Sweelinck and Lœillet; in Germany, Scheidt, Froberger, Pachelbel, Buxtehude, Kuhnau, Mattheson and Bach; in France, de Chambonnières, the Couperins, Rameau and Daquin; an immense literature, comprising thousands of compositions, preludes and toccatas, suites and partitas, transcriptions of vocal pieces, concertos, sonatas, not to mention innumerable accompaniments and concerted numbers. The harpsichord is, as Schaeffner said, 'a centripetal force'; or as Mattheson (1713) put it, 'the column on which all the rest supports itself'.

[1] The 'aimable enfant' whose instrument touched La Fontaine more than all the music of the opera *Isis*, was the harpsichordist Mademoiselle Certain.

In the first operas it was part of the orchestra. In his opera *L'Orfeo* (1607) Monteverdi asked for two harpsichords. Even after Gluck 'reformed' the opera – that is for over two centuries – the harpsichord maintained its position in the theatre as the instrument to accompany the recitative. On first nights it was generally played by the composer himself, who was called for the occasion the *maestro al cembalo*.

In old orchestral music it played no less important a part. In contrast with the piano, whose timbre blends badly with the orchestra, the tone of the harpsichord, feebler but cleaner and more incisive, stands out clearly from the orchestral texture (notably in Bach's concertos, in which the replacement of the harpsichord by the piano produces a disastrous effect). In the nineteenth century Rossini still recommended it in preference to the piano for the accompaniment of singing (we shall soon meet with the opposite opinion).

Like all instruments widely played, the harpsichord exercised an important influence on style, though only in the long run after it had outstripped its rivals. The 'harpsichord style' is particularly characterised by its ornaments, shakes, trills, mordents, inverse mordents, etc., intended to prolong the brief sonority of the mechanically plucked string and to supplement its deficiency of expression. Such ornamentation was easily executed on the harpsichord, but is more difficult, and less effective, on the heavier action of the modern piano.[1]

We must add to such ornaments the 'echo' effect: the same figure repeated twice, at the unison or at the octave, the first time *forte* on the lower keyboard, the second time *piano* on the upper keyboard (a notable example is in the last movement of Bach's *Ouverture* in B minor, S.831). This 'echo' effect was common in all the music of the seventeenth and eighteenth centuries, especially in the opera, and it is impossible to determine whether it originated with the harpsichord or whether the harpsichord borrowed it from other types of music. Finally, there was the liberal use of arpeggios, which were evidently inherited from lute music.

In the second half of the eighteenth century the harpsichord had reached its supreme perfection. The multiplication of stops enabled it to produce upwards of twenty combinations of timbre. Let us take as an example a big harpsichord with two keyboards by Hieronymus Albrecht Hass of Hamburg, of 1734, in the Musée du Conservatoire in

---

[1] The pianos in Mozart's time also suffered from this lack of sustaining power. Thus the musical ornaments in the works of Mozart and his contemporaries had the same purpose as those in compositions for the harpsichord. It was to be quite otherwise with Beethoven, Schumann and Chopin, whose least grace-note is full of significance.

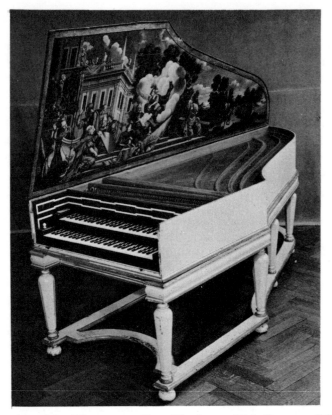

14 Harpsichord by Hieronymus Hass, Hamburg, 1734. Compass GG – d³. One set of strings of sixteen-foot pitch, two unisons of eight-foot, and one set of four-foot, operated by five rows of jacks (upper keyboard: eight-foot, lute; lower keyboard: sixteen-foot, two eight-foot, four-foot); there are buff stops to the lower manual sixteen-foot and eight-foot strings, and a coupler which, when the lower manual is pulled forwards, engages the lute stop on the upper manual. The stops are all placed within the instrument, above the wrest-plank. The sixteen-foot strings have their own, independent, soundboard outside the eight-foot hitch-pin rail. Note the double curve of the bent side, a speciality of Hamburg harpsichord makers, and the elaborate decoration of the keys (ivory naturals with arcaded fronts of ebony, accidentals inlaid with mother-of-pearl and tortoiseshell) and of the keyboard surround (tortoiseshell and ivory). This is one of the biggest harpsichords ever made – before the modern revival – and one of the very few old harpsichords to incorporate a sixteen-foot register. It was restored by Fleury in Paris in 1858. *Musée Instrumental du Conservatoire Royal de Musique, Brussels.*

Brussels (see plate 14). It is nearly nine feet long and has a compass of 4½ octaves from GG. There are four sets of strings, two unisons (at eight-foot pitch), one at sixteen-foot pitch, and one at four. There is a buff stop to the lower-manual eight-foot and sixteen-foot, a lute stop to the upper eight-foot, and a coupler.

However, the essential handicap of the instrument remained – its inability to provide subtle gradations of sound. Different degrees of dynamics could be produced, something which Bodky, alluding to the position of the two keyboards, picturesquely calls 'a terraced dynamic' – but intermediate shades of volume, *crescendo* and *diminuendo* were impossible.

This deficiency was strongly felt. In the maturity of the 'harpsichord style' an aspiration could be sensed towards a keyboard instrument capable of nuance. The expressive suppleness of the violin family offered an example to be envied. 'They [the violinists] can strike the string of their instrument as hard or as lightly as they wish, make it speak either loud or soft', complained Bénigne de Bacilly in 1679. In the preface to his first book of pieces for the harpsichord (1713) Couperin wrote: 'The harpsichord is perfect as to its range, and brilliant in its own right; but since it is impossible to increase or diminish the sound I shall always be grateful to those who, by infinite art supported by good taste, succeed in making the instrument capable of expression.'

Fifty years later in an article previously quoted from in a footnote (p. 39), Canon Trouflant wrote: 'By these means' – he is referring to stops – 'the executant could produce loud and soft tones, but the loud was always the same and the soft was always the same; there was no gradation from one to the other . . . . The builders were not the last to be aware of this imperfection, but they preferred sleep to the activity of genius, and made no effort to perfect this beautiful instrument, to enable it to execute the *forte, piano, amoroso, gustoso*, and all the other gradations of tone which appear with such charm in modern music.'

The desire for a more expressive keyboard instrument was so keen that some players anticipated its arrival. They claimed to produce differences in volume by variations in touch. Such players would assume facial expressions, poses and contortions of all kinds to give an impression of the nuance their instruments failed to produce. Composers made the same anticipations. In his Sonata with figured bass (1712) G. A. Piani wrote in *crescendo* and *diminuendo* signs.

The reproaches which Canon Trouflant had heaped upon the instrument builders were, however, unjust; for since the middle of the eighteenth century (and surely swayed by the heightened emotionalism

15 Harpsichord by Pascal Taskin, Paris, 1769. Compass FF – f³. Two strings
of eight foot pitch, and one of four, operated by three rows of jacks (upper
keyboard: eight-foot, quill, buff; lower keyboard: eight-foot, leather, buff,
four-foot, leather). A coupler enables the upper manual eight-foot to be
played from the lower keyboard. Note the soundboard, elaborately painted
in tempera, and the rose inscribed 'Pascal Taskin élève de Blancher'. This
harpsichord is believed to have been Taskin's personal instrument; it was
restored in 1882 by Louis Tomasini and soon after this lent to the Erards,
who, according to Raymond Russell, 'wished to copy it for commercial
production, and with this modern harpsichord-making began'. *Russell
Collection, Edinburgh.*

of this period which led to the dawning of romanticism) we see every effort being made to realise the Canon's desire. In 1766 in Paris, Virbès fitted to the harpsichord knee-pedals which drew back the jacks, like the *una corda, due corde* pedal of the piano.

What Canon Trouflant had praised most highly in Taskin's invention was, as we have seen, its capacity (very slight, in reality) for nuance. We have already mentioned Berger of Grenoble, who, in 1765, received from the Académie des Sciences a eulogy for his harpsichord which could produce *crescendi* and *decrescendi* by means of a 'lever' (pedal?), the mechanism of which was unfortunately not explained. In 1741 a Swede, Nils Brelin, had invented an upright harpsichord with eight pedals and sixty-one keys, with eight shades of volume from *piano* to *forte*. Milchmeyer's harpsichord, with three keyboards and 250·'changes' (1780), was planned with the same object in view. In 1769 Shudi patented in London his 'Venetian swell', an inner lid consisting of hinged slats which could be opened gradually by means of a pedal (a device similar to the swell box of the organ), and which could produce a *crescendo* and *decrescendo*. The less sophisticated 'Nag's head', a hinged flap along the bent side of the lid, patented by Kirckman, had a similar purpose.

But all these artifices, intended to make the plucked harpsichord sensitive to touch, were but expedients, incapable of curing its basic fault. It was the very method of setting the strings in vibration which had to be altered. Plucking had to give way to percussion; that is to say, the piano had to be created.

It appears, moreover, from contemporary documents, that the sole motive of the inventors of the piano – as its very name 'pianoforte' (Bartolomeo Cristofori's invention bore the name *'Gravicembalo col piano e forte'* – literally 'Harpsichord with soft and loud') indicates – was to remedy the harpsichord's inability to play loud and soft. (In much the same way Adolphe Sax, when he invented the saxophone, had at first in mind only the object of improving the clarinet by permitting it to 'octavate'.) They did not even change the name of the instrument. Marius, in Paris, gave to his invention the name 'hammer harpsichord'. In an eighteenth-century Italian manuscript it is called the *cembalo a martellini*, which means the same thing. And the German piano maker Schröter (inspired in his invention by his pupils who complained that their playing did not seem as expressive on the harpsichord as on the clavichord) only hoped to construct 'durable jacks'. Practically everywhere experiments of this sort were being made, experiments which in reality were all leading to the establishment of an entirely new

16 Harpsichord by Burkat Shudi and John Broadwood, London, 1775 (No. 762). Compass CC – f³. Two strings of eight-foot pitch, and one of four, operated by four rows of jacks (upper keyboard: eight-foot, lute; lower keyboard: two eight-foot, four-foot). A fifth lever (the third from the left above the upper keyboard) applies a buff stop to the eight-foot string operated by the lower keyboard only, and a sixth (on the inside of the left-hand cheek) engages the 'machine', whereby a pre-determined change of stop-combinations on both keyboards can be brought into play when the left pedal is depressed. The right pedal operates the Venetian swell (seen in its open position in the photograph). The case is of mahogany. The instrument, which is a fine example of the classical English harpsichord at the peak of its development, once belonged to Joseph Haydn. *Kunsthistorisches Museum, Vienna.*

principle – that of the piano.

The piano by no means established its popularity without resistance. The harpsichord had its convinced defenders who found an eloquent argument in the sometimes crude sound of primitive pianos; that 'coppersmith's instrument' as Voltaire wrote to Madame du Deffand in 1774. When Taskin had the honour of playing the first piano at the Tuileries before the Queen, Balbastre said to him: 'Never will this newcomer dethrone the majestic harpsichord'. Canon Trouflant, the prophet of the harpsichord à buffle, wrote in 1774: 'If you glance attentively at its [the piano's] construction its complexity terrifies. If the treble is charming, the bass, hard, muffled and false, sickens our French ears.'

Even eleven years later the Encyclopédie (Art of the Instrument Maker) which devotes many pages to the construction of the harpsichord and the organ, says nothing about the construction of the piano, and the 'Vocabulaire' at the end of the volume dismisses the newcomer as follows: 'Forte-piano or hammer-harpsichord: a small harpsichord of an oblong form, in which each key raises a kind of hammer of cardboard covered with leather, which strikes against two unison strings or against a single string'. In Germany, Schröter's new hammer instrument met only with irony and scepticism. Silbermann was not less criticised, and we shall see that Bach would have nothing to do with his instrument, any more than Handel who, sojourning in Florence in 1709, must have had the opportunity to become acquainted with Cristofori's first efforts.

Nevertheless, the days of the harpsichord were numbered. In spite of all resistance, in spite of the difficulties of adopting a new technique, the piano was inevitably victorious. Harpsichords were even converted into pianos; of eight old pianos in the museums in Berlin, five are so converted. In Italy the evolution was accomplished before the last quarter of the eighteenth century. At least this is the impression which Dr Burney gives. During his visit to Italy in 1770, he found the harpsichord so neglected both by makers and players that it was difficult to say which was worse, the instruments or the performers. 'To persons accustomed to English harpsichords, all the keyed instruments on the continent appear to great disadvantage. Throughout Italy they have generally little octave spinets to accompany singing, in private houses, sometimes in a triangular form, but more frequently in the shape of our old virginals; of which the keys are so noisy, and the tone so feeble, that more wood is heard than wire. The best Italian harpsichord which I met with for touch, was that of Signor Grimani at Venice; and for tone, that of Monsignor Reggio at Rome; but I found three English harpsichords in the three principal cities of Italy, which are regarded by the Italians as so many phenomena. One was made by Shudi, and is in the possession of the Hon. Mrs Hamilton at Naples. The other two, which are of Kirckman's make, belong to Mrs Richie at Venice, and to the Hon. Mrs Earl, who resided at Rome when I was there.'

In France the struggle between the two instruments was short but lively. We see first the professionals, then the amateurs abandon the old instrument for the new. Advertisers asked 'to trade an excellent harpsichord against a piano'. The decisive moment came with the Revolution. The aristocratic harpsichord, the instrument of an over-refined society, was swept away in the tumult. When the new bourgeois society was finally established, its instrument was no longer the harpsichord, but the more striking piano, the 'harmonious ivory' as Delille called it. The regulations of the Conservatoire de Paris in 1795 still provided for six professors of the harpsichord. A prize for this instrument was awarded for the last time in 1798.[1] After that it was replaced by a prize for the piano. (The first professor of the new piano course was Boieldieu.)

For nearly a century the harpsichord was to sink into oblivion. In Western Europe even its literature was to be forgotten. The eventual revival of this literature towards the last quarter of the nineteenth century did not bring with it a revival of the harpsichord, the works of Bach, Scarlatti and Rameau being invariably executed on the piano. In 1880, Mendel-Reissmann's *Musikalisches Konversationslexikon* stated bluntly that 'today the harpsichord is scarcely known'.

But the rebirth of the old instrument was to come soon. Together with the *viola da gamba* and the *viola d'amore*, it was the first to benefit from the movement in favour of restoring ancient music in its authentic colour, that is to say on the instruments of its time, instead of approximate reconstructions on their modern successors. It reappeared even in the orchestra. Falla and Poulenc both wrote concertos for it (in 1926 and 1928 respectively) and the former used it in his puppet opera *El retablo de Maese Pedro* (1923) Thanks largely to the example and influence of Wanda Landowska (1879-1959) the instrument is now fully restored to its former status and prestige.

Makers of spinets and harpsichords were legion. In Italy we may name from the end of the fifteenth century, Giovanni Spinetti and Baffo

---

[1] A poem on Music, composed in Paris in this same year, contained these lines:
' . . . Soon the first harpsichord was fashioned.
For so long the instrument enjoyed a happy destiny;
Attaining today the decline of its age,
It leaves the piano its superb heritage.'

17   Harpsichord by Jacob and Abraham Kirckman, London, 1776. Compass FF – f³, but without FF♯ . The disposition is similar to that of the Shudi and Broadwood harpsichord of 1775 (plate 16), except that, unusually, the buff stop operates on the upper keyboard eight-foot strings (as well as the lute stop). The case is of mahogany and the lid incorporates a 'Nag's head' or movable flap, which, like Shudi's Venetian swell, is operated by the right pedal, and of which the mechanism can be seen in the photograph. *Victoria and Albert Museum, London.*

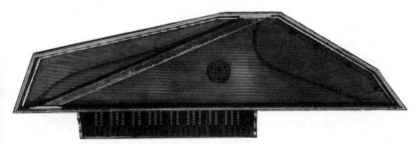

18   Spinet, unsigned (Italian, *c* 1575). Compass GG – c³, with short octave. The instrument is of cypress wood, and has, characteristically, an outer case (though of later date, and not shown in this photograph) to protect it, but from which it could be removed, if required, for playing. It is a fine example of the hexagonal Italian spinet, with its projecting keyboard, and is traditionally supposed to have belonged to Queen Elizabeth I of England. *Victoria and Albert Museum, London.*

of Venice, Rossi of Milan, Zanetti, Tacani, Farini (who also employed gut strings) and Cristofori of Florence, Girolamo Zenti of Rome, to whom we may add the Netherlanders established in Italy, especially in Rome, such as 'Mattia di Gand, fiammingo – considered as an equal of the best Italians'; in Germany, J. N. Bach of Iena, J. G. Gleichmann of Erfurt, Z. Hildebrand of Leipzig, Hass of Hamburg and Gottfried Silbermann of Freiburg.

The French were no less active in the same field. C. Pierre names seven makers in the seventeenth century and forty-nine in the eighteenth. We cite Richard-Jean Denis, Cuisiner, the Blanchets (three generations, F. E., A. F. N., P. A. C., this last a piano builder), Nicolas Dumont – who is said to have built in Paris the first harpsichord with five octaves – and Taskin.[1]

In England where an immense virginal literature had grown up there were: Thomas Barton, William Pether, the Hitchcock family, John Loosemore, Stephen Keen, Gabriell Townsend (who built for Elizabeth Stuart, ephemeral Queen of Bohemia, an instrument which is now in the Brussels Museum), the Haywards, Hermann Tabel, Jacob Kirckman and the Swiss Shudi (or Tschudi), successors to Tabel, whom we shall meet again in the history of the piano. Shudi came to London in 1718 and was an intimate of Handel. The child Mozart played an instrument Shudi made for Frederick II.

At the end of the eighteenth century the manufacture of harpsichords was introduced into the United States, especially by Benjamin Crehore.

From the end of the sixteenth to the middle of the seventeenth century (that is, during the great period of Flemish art) harpsichord building was centred in Antwerp. The builders were attached, as we have already said, to the Guild of St Luke, in which, because of their great number, they formed a special section with their own special regulations. The names of about fifty such builders are known, the most famous being the Ruckers, Hans called 'the Elder' (c. 1550-1625) and his son Hans or Jean 'the Younger' (1578-1642), Andreas 'the Elder' (1597-c.1655) and finally his son Andreas 'the Younger' (1607-?).

Hans the Elder, originally a simple carpenter, was a native of Malines.

---

[1] It was a German harpsichord-maker established in Paris, Tobias Schmidt, who was charged with the construction of the 'beheading machine' unjustly called the guillotine, ordered in 1789 by the Assembly on the recommendation of Dr Guillotin to replace the barbarous use of the axe. Schmidt made a fortune 'in the enterprise of construction with which he had been charged', supplying guillotines to every department of the Republic. Falling in love with 'La Chameroi', a danseuse officially protected by Euguène de Beauharnais, the former harpsichord-maker quickly saw his curiously acquired fortune melt away (Lenôtre, *La Révolution par ceux qui l'ont vue*).

19 Double Virginal by Hans Ruckers the Elder, Antwerp, 1581. Compass C
– c³, and c – c⁴, with short octave. The case is of oak and bears the
characteristic Ruckers block-printed paper decoration, with a painting on
the interior of the lid. The smaller instrument, an octave higher in pitch
than the main one, is fitted like a drawer, and can be removed and placed
on top of the main instrument, giving the effect of a two-manual
instrument. The original stand is missing. *Metropolitan Museum of Art,
New York* (Gift of B. H. Homan, 1929).

The oldest existing harpsichords built by him are dated 1590. The
Ruckers produced an incredible number of instruments which they sent
all over the world. Well over one hundred of them are still preserved
in the museums of Europe and America.[1] A number of years ago a
double virginal of 1581 by Hans Ruckers was discovered in Peru (it is
now in the Metroplitan Museum in New York); possibly it was
imported into Peru at the time of the Spanish Conquest (plate 19).

At the end of the eighteenth century the vogue of the Ruckers in
Paris was so great that people preferred to have an old Ruckers

---

[1] The *Encyclopédie*, 1785, says: 'The best harpsichords that we have had up to now for the beauty
of their tone are those of the three Ruckers, Hans, Jean and Andreas, and of Jean Couchet who,
all established in Antwerp during the last century, have made an immense quantity of harpsichords
of which a great many are in Paris. There are builders who have copied or counterfeited the
harpsichords of the Ruckers so well that they may be mistaken for genuine Ruckers instruments
from their exteriors, but the quality of their tone always betrays them.'

harpsichord rebuilt rather than to buy a new instrument made by another builder. We have already seen how Taskin spent much of his time in these transformations or *ravalements*. Among the instruments seized from the *émigrés* by the French Revolution authorities, six Ruckers were identified. It is to the Ruckers that Hüllmandel in his article *Harpsichord* in the *Encyclopédie Méthodique* attributed the idea of coupling two strings in unison with a third, shorter, tuned an octave higher, as well as the use of brass strings for the bass and steel strings for the treble, the invention of the second keyboard, the extension of the keyboard to four octaves, and the tapering of the soundboard to accord with the pitch of the strings. Many of these claims are, however, flagrantly false; Virdung, in 1511, already knew keyboards of four octaves as well as the use of brass with steel strings.

In addition to the Ruckers the Couchets deserve special mention. They was also a dynasty, related to the Ruckers, particularly the first Jean, a nephew of Jean Ruckers the younger, who delivered a harpsichord to de Chambonnières, harpsichordist and organist to the King in Paris, and one of the founders of the French harpsichord school.[1]

Among sixteenth-century builders were also Gilles Brebos, Jacob Moors and their sons, Hans Bos, Jean Grouwels, Joost Kareest who came from Cologne, and Van der Biest. In the seventeenth century there was Georges Britsen; in the eighteenth, Johann Daniel Dulcken – not to be confused with Johann Ludwig Dulcken, instrument maker to the court of Munich, who at the time of the Antwerp School's decadence came to Brussels.[2]

At the same time a Brussels builder named Bremers was the first there to fit the jacks *à buffle*. In the Walloon provinces during the eighteenth century we note the names of Albert Delin of Tournai and especially of Pascal Taskin.

Old harpsichords are difficult to keep regulated and in tune, and the manufacture of new instruments has been taken up again today on a fairly large scale, both by established piano manufacturers and by craftsmen working at home. These modern harpsichords are generally very successful, copied from ancient models and modernised only in their accessory parts, particularly by the substitution of multiple pedals for the clumsy hand stops.

---

[1] This fact is related by Henri Dumont, director of music at the Chapelle Royale, Paris, who described the instrument as 'a spinet with two keyboards which is so excellent that I do not believe anyone after poor Couchet could make another like it'.

[2] At this time Burney noted that the Antwerp harpsichords were inferior to the English.

20 Virginal by Thomas White, London, 1642. Compass C – c³. The case is of oak. This is a typical example of the English seventeenth-century virginal, with its inset keyboard and its convex lid, painted inside, which was certainly influenced by the Flemish instruments imported into England in the early years of the century. Comparison with the Italian spinet (plate 18) also shows the similar layout of the two instruments, despite the fact that in the English one the case is projected to form a rectangle. *Victoria and Albert Museum, London.*

21 Virginal by Gabriell Townsend, (?) London, 1641. Compass C – e³. The case is of oak, decorated with paintings and bearing the Plantagenet Royal Arms. The instrument belonged to Elizabeth Stuart, Queen of Bohemia, daughter of King James I, and is the oldest surviving English virginal. *Musée Instrumental du Conservatoire Royal de Musique, Brussels.*

Since harpsichords were not easily transformed into pianos[1] most of the ancient instruments were destroyed (especially in order to rob them of their decorations) or else suffered strange fates. Some years ago one was discovered in a farmhouse in Brabant acting as a side-table in the dining-room. The greatest and most regrettable destruction was perpetrated in Paris at the beginning of the Restoration. The instruments seized from the *émigrés* had been stored in the attics of the Royal School of Singing which had become the Paris Conservatoire. There were three hundred and sixty-seven instruments there, about a hundred of them harpsichords. In 1816 the Conservatoire was moved into the ancient quarters of the 'Menus' and on this occasion an inventory of the instruments was made (*State of the Instruments taken from the Dépôt National, rue Bergère, to the Conservatoire, established at the Menus*). This document was published by Gallay in 1890 (*An Inventory under the Terror*). Lack of money prevented the Directors from acquiring sufficient wood to heat the Conservatoire during the particularly rigorous winter of 1816, and the harpsichords were burned to provide warmth.

Unfortunately, most surviving old harpsichords betray signs of rebuilding and of alterations generally unhappy, sometimes recent, but more often old. Often the quills have been replaced with leather, the stops multiplied, the cases lengthened, the decoration 'improved' to meet the taste of the day. (The organist Balbastre possessed a Ruckers – sixteenth or seventeenth century – which had been decorated with the chief scenes from Rameau's opera *Castor et Pollux,* 1737.) The handsome and massive straight stands of the seventeenth century are replaced by slender claw-foot stands.

In extreme cases successive alterations finally altered the old instruments so radically that, to quote the *Encyclopédie,* 'nothing was left of the original instrument but the soundboard'. It would, however, be a mistake further to alter these alterations, which are themselves already old, in order to restore the instruments to their original appearance. Time, which harmonises everything, has already consecrated such anachronisms, which are like a Renaissance altar in a Gothic church.

Before leaving the harpsichord, we should mention some of its variants, variants often as fantastic as those the piano has in its time inspired. The quarter-tone harpsichord of Vicentino has already been

[1] A two-manual harpsichord of 1608 by Andreas Ruckers, formerly belonging to Raymond Russell, had been converted to a piano in the eighteenth century, and was subsequently turned back into a harpsichord by Hugh Gough. The Metropolitan Museum of Art in New York possesses a harpsichord made in Paris in 1754 by Jean Goermans, transformed into a piano later in the century. (Ed.)

22 Spinet by John Player, London, *c* 1775. Compass GG – c^3, with short octave. The case is of oak. Player was apprenticed to Gabriell Townsend (see plate 21) for seven years, from 1650 to 1657, and his earliest surviving instrument is a virginal in the style of his master. This spinet, in a form that was to prove popular in England throughout most of the eighteenth century, is therefore doubly interesting for having been built by a maker brought up in the sixteenth-century virginal tradition, and as one of the earliest examples of a new form of small, domestic harpsichord that was to occupy a position comparable to that of the upright piano. *Victoria and Albert Museum, London.*

23 Interior view of the same instrument. The difference of the design from
that of the Italian spinet or the Flemish and English virginal can clearly
be seen, the jacks in the older instruments being set at an acute angle from
the keyboard, with the wrest-pins on the right, but here following the line
of the keyboard, so that the instrument is virtually a harpsichord confined
within a small space. This accounts for the instrument's characteristic, and
elegant, wing-shaped appearance. *Victoria and Albert Museum, London.*

referred to (see page 47). A similar instrument, constructed in 1548 in
Venice by Domenico Pisaurensis for the acoustician Zarlino, divided
every whole tone into four parts. Then there were the enharmonic
instruments of Luzzaschi of Ferrara (1597) and of Trasuntino of Venice
(1606) as well as the 'universal clavicymbalum' constructed in Prague
in 1588 by Karl Luyton, which Prætorius in his *Syntagma musicum* says
he saw in Vienna.

Hans Ruckers made instruments which combined in a single rectangular case a two-manual harpsichord and a spinet. Transposing
instruments were made, which were particularly useful (or even indispensable) at a time when pitch was so variable. These transposing
instruments utilised the upper manual for the purpose.

68

The harpsichord was combined with other instruments, notably with the organ in the *claviorganum*, or 'organised harpsichord' (see plate 9), first constructed in Italy in the sixteenth century and taken up again in England, France and Germany.

Bach had a lute-harpsichord made by Zacharias Hildebrand, furnished with two sets of gut strings, the tone of which was said to deceive even lute-players, and for which he composed a Prelude, Fugue and Allegro in E flat, S. 998. In Paris an 'angelic harpsichord' was made, with jacks tipped with leather covered with velvet. 'Pedal-harpsichords' were built for home organ practice. A 'mechanical harpsichord' with two keyboards, made by Sébastien Erard for Monsieur de la Blancherie, was much admired.

We should add also the old keyboard stringed instruments which shared with the harpsichord only its name, instruments in which the plucking of the strings was replaced by mechanical friction. Their prototype seems to have been the *Geigenwerk* of Hans Heiden of Nuremberg (1625), a sort of big viol with a keyboard, shaped like a grand piano, and furnished with four wheels emerging from the soundboard, worked by a crank, against which the strings were lowered when the keys were depressed. This instrument was copied immediately afterwards in Spain (by Raymundo Truchador), in France (by Cusinier, who built a *clavecin-vielle* in 1708, perfecting it in 1734, and by Le Voir in 1741), and in Germany (by Hohlfeld's *Bogenflügel*, where the string was continuously stroked by a little sachet filled with resin). The *Bogenflügel*, presented to Frederick the Great in 1754 and admired by C. P. E. Bach, had a certain success. The same principle was applied in about 1760, by Renaud to his spinet with a continuous horsehair bow.

Finally there were certain purely fantastic instruments: the 'orchestra-harpsichord' (1724) of Piechbeck, an Englishman, which is said (by Gerber) to have had flute, trumpet and drum attachments; the monstrous apparatus with 790 strings and 130 registers (one of which produced an electric shock!) rigged up in 1730 by a certain Pastor Dewin; another by the Wagner brothers in Schmiedefeld (1764) with a flute stop; one by an English mechanic in 1768 with drums and trumpet; the 'acoustic harpsichord' of Virbès of Paris in 1771, which he took around the French provinces, imitating an entire orchestra. We shall come across many of these fantasies again in the piano.

Even the size and shape of the harpsichord was varied, extended, reduced, pulled about in every sense of the word. Tiny spinets were made which shut up to look like a Bible. From 1700 the Parisian builder Marius made harpsichords *de voyage*, which folded in three sections, of which an example, owned by Frederick the Great and carried by him on his campaigns, is now in Berlin.

3 *The Piano*

With the piano we return to the principle of the 'struck' string, as in the clavichord; but this time by a system infinitely more advanced, one which increased both the instrument's dynamic range and its sustaining power. For this a hammer was needed, a hammer which, having struck the string, immediately disengaged itself, simultaneously with a damper, both afterwards returning to their original position. Hence the mechanical complexity of the piano, a complexity which today would appear to have been developed to its furthest limits.

The basic piano action requires a hammer which is activated by a lever or pusher (either fixed or movable), called – by analogy with the harpsichord – a 'jack', attached to the key beyond its fulcrum. When the key is depressed the jack rises and throws the hammer against the string. When the key is released (and only then), the hammer falls back into position. Inevitably, this system, however well designed, presents serious disadvantages. In order to prevent the jack, by its swift action, from breaking the shank of the hammer and also to prevent the hammer from rebounding from the jack and hitting the string a second

71

time ('blocking'), it is necessary to keep the hammer at some distance from the string. Therefore, in order to give the hammer sufficient impetus, the key has to be struck firmly, and time must be allowed to permit the hammer to fall back into place, which means that a soft touch and rapid repetition are both impossible. These two disadvantages are overcome by an ancillary device known as the escapement,[1] which allows the hammer to disengage itself from the jack after striking the string.[2]

The unconscious inspirer of the piano may have been Pantaleon Hebenstreit (1669-1750) who, having perfected the ancient dulcimer in an instrument called after his own first name, attracted public attention to the tonal properties of the struck string. The Pantaleon was praised by well-known musicians. Its powers of expressiveness and nuance were widely admired, but the labour of striking its strings by hand-mallets was (according to Kuhnau) 'herculean'. Some sort of mechanism was needed. In the space of eight years, this need was supplied successively by three men of three different nationalities apparently unknown to each other. These men were Cristofori of Florence in 1709, Marius of Paris in 1716, and Schröter of Dresden in 1717. The first inventor was thus Bartolomeo Cristofori (Padua, 1651 – Florence, 1731), a repairer and tuner of harpsichords in the service of Prince Ferdinando de' Medici, Grand Duke of Tuscany, and Keeper of his instrumental collection.

Cristofori's action (described with drawings in the *Giornale de' litterati d'Italia,* 1711) is extremely simple, but it contains all the essentials of the system: the hinged hammer independent of the key (with its escapement), which falls back after striking the string which it allows to vibrate freely, the hammer check, and the damper – one for each string (see Appendix, Figure 4). Just as the clavichord in some ways anticipated the piano, Cristofori's primitive escapement mechanism anticipated Erard's more sophisticated double escapement, which, in the final analysis, is not a new conception, but merely the technical perfection of the earlier Italian invention.

In 1720 Cristofori notably improved his action. He also invented a mechanism still employed in modern piano building: the shift of the keyboard by means of the soft pedal, so that the hammer strikes only

---

[1] The word 'escapement' is incorrectly applied to this most important part of the piano mechanism, since in the piano the word describes not the activity itself, but the part. Actually the escapement 'escapes' from the hammer after it has struck the string, and might more accurately be called the 'escaper'.

[2] For a more detailed account of the evolution of piano action see Rosamond Harding's *The Piano-Forte, a History* (1933) and her article in Grove's *Dictionary of Music and Musicians* (1954). (Ed.)

24 Grand pianoforte by Bartolomeo Cristofori, Florence, 1720. Compass C –
f³ Bichord. A *una corda* effect can be obtained by sliding the keyboard and
keyframe leftwards (using the ivory knobs at each end). This is the older
of the two surviving pianos made by Cristofori and therefore the earliest
piano in existence. Comparison with the Baffo harpsichord (plate 7) will
show that Cristofori followed traditional harpsichord design for the case
of his new instrument, although the action itself was revolutionary.
Metropolitan Museum of Art, New York (The Crosby Brown Collection of
Musical Instruments, 1889).

one string instead of two, or two strings instead of three (*una corda, due
corde*); but as the pedal had not yet been thought of, the mechanism
was worked by means of knobs fixed at each end of the keyboard. To
the instrument itself Cristofori had given the shape of the harpsichord and he called it *gravicembalo col piano e forte* ('harpsichord
with soft and loud') an expression already used in the sixteenth century
in Venice by Giovanni Gabrieli in his *Sonata pian' e forte* for strings and
brass. The two adjectives, contracted, became the standard name of the
instrument, the pianoforte, widely contracted to piano. (It is the same

word in English, French and Portuguese; in German[1] it is once again *the klavier*).

As in the case of equal temperament, composers were found immediately to put into practice the resources of the new instrument: first Lodovico Giustini in a sonata 'for soft and loud harpsichord, commonly called mallet-harpsichord' (Pistoia, 1731) and in twelve sonatas *per piano e forte,* with expression marks (Florence, 1732, republished by Rosamond Harding, London, 1933). But Cristofori derived little profit from his genius. He built few pianos and had to go back to making harpsichords. Only two of his instruments have been preserved, one (of 1720) in the Metropolitan Museum of Art in New York (see plate 24), and the other (of 1726) in the Karl-Marx-Universität in Leipzig. In passing, we may note that in Goethe's time a piano by Cristofori was in use in Weimar.

The other two presumed inventors of the piano were no more fortunate. Jean Marius, of whose life we know nothing, but to whom Fétis and other authorities attribute the invention of the new principle, presented in 1716 to the Académie des Sciences four projects for a *clavecin à maillets (i.e.* a harpsichord with mallets) with a mechanism much more rudimentary than Cristofori's. In the first of Marius' schemes, the hammer, being part of the key, came up under the string which it struck when the key was depressed; there was no damper and no escapement. The second showed several series of mallets striking the strings either from beneath or from above. Thus, from the very origins of the piano, we see the hesitation between these two arrangements. In spite of the obvious superiority of striking the strings from beneath, eminent builders like Streicher of Vienna (1823), Hildebrandt of Leipzig, and Pape of Paris (1825), all used the opposite system, for a time at least.[2]

In Marius' third project, the hammer is replaced by a vertical jack supplied, not with a quill, but with a pin to strike the string. His final scheme combines, by means of two keyboards, the piano with the harpsichord. In the succession of Marius' four methods, it is not hard

---

[1] At first the German word was *hammerklavier,* literally 'keyboard instrument with hammers'. But the word was little used, the disappearance of the harpsichord rendering confusion impossible. For a while the meaning of the word *hammerklavier* was even uncertain. When Beethoven in 1818 used it in the title of his Sonata in B flat, Op. 106, he asked his editor whether the word should be *hammerklavier* or *hammerflügel.*

[2] The down-striking action does, however, have the advantage that the soundboard and the wrest-plank can be built as a unit, without the need for a gap between them through which the hammers can reach the strings (which necessitates bracing to counteract the tension of the strings). (Ed.)

74

to observe a discouraging return to the principle of the plucked string. It is said that none of his designs was actually put into practice, but we cannot be sure of this. All we know is that Marius disappeared, forgotten, and that it was from England and Germany that France received the new instrument.

The first German piano maker was as unlucky as Marius. It was in 1721 that Christoph Gottlieb Schröter presented to the Elector of Saxony in Dresden two piano actions, hoping that the Prince would furnish him with the means of applying his invention. His hopes were not realised. He then committed the imprudence of publicly exhibiting his models; others hastened to execute them, though without success. In a long article Schröter bitterly claimed priority for his invention, certain details of which recall Cristofori's instrument. It is not improbable that he knew about the *gravicembalo col piano e forte*. Schröter's hammer, hinged on a pin, is put into action by a jack perpendicular to the key. When the key is depressed, the jack strikes the hammer and throws it against the string. One of his projects places the hammer above the string, another below. His action did not provide for a damper, which Lenker of Rudolstadt added to it in 1765.[1]

Like Cristofori and Marius, Schröter made no profit from his invention, and, as is often the case, it was a newcomer who benefited from their efforts. The first man who exploited the piano industrially and with success, was the organ builder Gottfried Silbermann of Klein-Bobritzsch in Saxony (1683-1753) who established himself later in Freiberg. In France they even attributed the invention of the 'hammer-harpsichord' to him. Silbermann's action, constructed in 1726, was influenced both by Cristofori and Schröter. It was not his first effort as a copyist; he had previously had words with Hebenstreit whose Pantaleon he had imitated. A description of Cristofori's instrument had appeared in Germany in 1725 in Mattheson's musical journal, *Critica Musica,* and again seven years later in Walther's *Musical Dictionary.*

But Silbermann's action resembled rather the improved model which Cristofori had made in 1720, and it is probable that he had seen an instrument of this later type. Silbermann's action had no dampers in the proper sense of the word; he replaced them by a kind of mop-stick fringed with wool which rested on the strings, against which the mop-stick could be pressed as hard as desired by means of stops. Later

[1] Descriptions and plans of the actions of Cristofori (1711 and 1720), Marius and Schröter are reproduced in full in an essay by Leo Puliti entitled *Cenni storici della vita del serenissimo Ferdinando dei Medicis, granprincipe di Toscana, e della origine del pianoforte,* presented at a meeting of the Musical Academy of Florence in 1875 and published in the Academy's *Acta.* It is among the most important of the many studies devoted to this subject.

this mop-stick was divided into several hinged sections permitting separate parts of the keyboard to be damped. Imported into England, Silbermann's action later became known as the 'English action'.

Silbermann's instruments, luckier than their predecessors, aroused the liveliest interest, and their maker received the active support of Frederick the Great. That music-loving monarch, a partisan of all new ideas, was enthusiastic about the new system, and bought from Silbermann seven·pianos at once for seven hundred thalers each, a handsome price for those times. Silbermann was less successful with J. S. Bach, to whom he submitted his invention for the first time in 1726. Bach criticised the feebleness of the upper notes and the heaviness of the action. Though hurt by this rebuff, Silbermann did not forget Bach's advice, and two years afterwards again presented to him a modified and improved form of his instrument. This time Bach declared himself satisfied; but he remained faithful to the harpsichord just the same. The hour of the piano's triumph had not yet arrived. Though it is said that the need creates the instrument, it almost seems in the case of the piano that the instrument preceded the need. Cristofori's invention had come too soon. The style which was to make it useful, and soon indispensable, was not to become established until the second half of the eighteenth century.

At this time the style of musical writing underwent a profound change. The polyphony of Bach gave way to broadly developed melody, supported by a subordinate accompaniment. The more emotional generation of that time demanded a more expressive kind of music, with subtle gradations of volume unknown in the preceding era. Haydn and Mozart are the outstanding geniuses of this movement which led to the ardent lyricism of Beethoven.

We have already seen that this evolution, at the same time musical and psychological, resulted in the unexpected renaissance of the clavichord's popularity. But the clavichord was no match for its young rival. The piano was soon to develop to the extreme that capacity for nuance which had given to the clavichord itself its only advantage over the harpsichord. In the first part of his treatise, C. P. E. Bach, though speaking of the piano with an insistence which attests to its growing importance, still clearly preferred the clavichord. But only a few years later Frederick the Great's *Kammercembalist*, in the second part of the same treatise, pointed out that the piano was indispensable for the accompaniment of song, especially in the theatre, and even as a solo instrument for free improvisation. The piano was also more appropriate than the harpsichord for transcriptions of the orchestral works of the

Mannheim School and their contemporaries, whose compositions were more highly coloured than the older classics.

The work of Silbermann was continued by his nephew, Johann Heinrich (1727-99), under whom the firm acquired a European renown. A whole series of innovations, both for the organ and the piano, was credited to the Silbermanns, sometimes to Gottfried and sometimes to Johann Heinrich, recalling the fame of the Ruckers in the days gone by.

By this time the piano had become indispensable, and in spite of its rudimentary state compared with the refinement of the last harpsichords, and in spite of the desperate protests of the last defenders of the old instrument, it imposed itself victoriously – as the fifteenth century artillery had triumphed over the ancient crossbow, perfected though it too had been. We have quoted the laconic notice with which the *Encyclopédie* had dismissed the new instrument under the heading *Harpsichord*. The musical dictionary of the *Encyclopédie méthodique*, which appeared thirty years later, contains in contrast under the word *Pianoforte* a panegyric upon the new instrument by the Belgian theorist de Momigny (1762-1838), one of the most advanced musical spirits of his age. What Momigny praises in the piano is above all its expressiveness. 'It has this advantage', he writes, 'that the pressure of the finger determines the strength or weakness of the sound: thus it lends itself to expression and to the player's feelings. . . . It receives from the pianist's touch a kind of magic animation which causes the tone to take on every character. . . . It is particularly suited to pieces whose pathos is stressed by the harmony. It is accused of being tiring to play because the hammer fatigues the fingers. Nevertheless, we notice that the majority of the masters prefer this instrument for their compositions because it gives them more marked effects than does the harpsichord.'

In Germany, the piano, once it became known, spread no less rapidly. Gluck used it. From the moment that Mozart in 1777 discovered the pianos of Stein, he definitely gave up the harpsichord as a solo instrument. Haydn did the same, and for stronger reasons, so did Beethoven. A letter in *Cramer's Magazine,* addressed from Bonn in 1787, says: 'The piano is greatly admired here. We have several instruments by Stein of Augsburg. . . . The young Baron von Gudenau plays the pianoforte splendidly and so does the young Beethoven.'

The words 'for harpsichord or piano' which appear in the original title-pages of many of Beethoven's Sonatas were intended . by the publishers to attract that amateur clientèle who still owned harpsichords. The title which Beethoven gave to his Op. 106, *Sonate für das Hammerclavier,* has sometimes been interpreted to mean that the works written before were intended for the harpsichord, or at least for either instrument. This is not the case. The explanation is that Beethoven, at the time when he composed the sonata (1818) was going through a phase of Germanic purism which led him into the affectation of substituting German musical terminology for the normal Italian.

And so we see, during the second half of the eighteenth century, piano makers multiplying in Germany, from which country, however, a great many emigrated because of the Seven Years War, carrying their industry abroad, particularly to England.

The first period of the piano's prosperity as well as the first period of German manufacture is personified in the figure of a workman and disciple of Silbermann: Johann Andreas Stein (1728-1792) of Heidesheim, who set up in Augsburg as an organ builder. It may be remarked that the first German piano makers were organ builders, special workshops for the newer instruments not appearing until about 1730. Stein abandoned organ building later to devote himself entirely to the piano. It was when passing through Augsburg in 1777 that Mozart made the acquaintance of Stein's pianos which he adopted at once.

On the advice of his father, Mozart presented himself to Stein *incognito,* taking care to talk much about another builder named Friederici of whom Stein was jealous. In a long letter to Leopold Mozart the young master has much to say about Stein's pianos, praising their qualities highly and enumerating one after the other all the details of their mechanism.

'This time I shall begin at once with Stein's pianofortes. Before I had seen any of his make, Späth's claviers had always been my favourites. But now I much prefer Stein's for they damp ever so much better than the Regensburg instruments. When I strike hard, I can keep my finger on the note or raise it, but the sound ceases the moment I have produced it. In whatever way I touch the keys, the tone is always even. It never jars, it is never stronger or weaker or entirely absent; in a word, it is always even. It is true that he does not sell a pianoforte of this kind for less than three hundred gulden, but the trouble and labour which Stein puts into the making of it cannot be paid for. His instruments have this special advantage over others that they are made with escape action. Only one maker in a hundred bothers about this. But without an escapement it is impossible to avoid jangling and vibration after the note is struck. When you touch the keys, the hammers fall back again the moment after they have struck the strings, whether you hold down the keys or release them. He himself told me that when he has finished making one of

25 Grand pianoforte by Johann Andreas Stein, Augsburg, 1786. Compass FF
– f³. Bichord. Two knee pedals (*genouillères*) control, respectively, the
dampers and the 'piano' (*una corda*) shift. Note the graceful curve of the
tail, the inclined angle of the keyboard 'fall', and the elegant tapering legs.
Musée Instrumental du Conservatoire Royal de Musique, Brussels.

these claviers, he sits down to it and tries all kinds of passages, runs and jumps, and he polishes and works at it until it can do anything. For he labours solely in the interest of music and not for his own profit: otherwise he would soon finish his work. He often says: "If I were not myself such a passionate lover of music, and had not myself some slight skill on the clavier, I should certainly long ago have lost patience with my work. But I do like an instrument which never lets the player down and which is durable." And his claviers certainly do last. He guarantees that the soundboard will neither break nor split. When he has finished making one for a clavier, he places it in the open air, exposing it to rain, snow, the heat of the sun and all the devils in order that it may crack. Then he inserts wedges and glues them in to make the instrument very strong and firm. He is delighted when it cracks, for he can then be sure that nothing more can happen to it. Indeed he often cuts into it himself and then glues it together again and strengthens it in this way.'

Ten years later in 1787 the young Beethoven, returning from his first trip to Vienna, passed through Augsburg and also visited the Stein family.

Stein perfected what is known as the 'German' or 'Viennese' action (see Appendix, Figure 6), which differed from the 'English' action (derived from Cristofori) in that the hammer, instead of facing away from the player and being hinged to a frame above the keys, is attached to the far end of the key, pivoting in a sheath (the *kapsel*) and facing towards the player. When the key is depressed the projecting butt of the hammer engages with a rail (the *prelleiste*) behind the keys and is so jerked upwards to the string. In the more advanced form of the German action the *prelleiste* itself incorporated an escapement mechanism.

The Musée du Conservatoire in Brussels has one of the rare surviving Stein pianos (see plate 25). Its hammers are covered with chamois leather and are scarcely larger than peas; its tone is gentle, its timbre thin but clear and distinguished; the strings are of steel in the treble, and of unwrapped brass in the bass (as in the harpsichord, which the instrument somewhat recalls both in tone and appearance). Instead of pedals it is furnished with 'knee-pedals' or *genouillères*, which raise the dampers. The outstanding characteristic of the instrument is the lightness of its action compared with that of a modern piano, the keys being depressed by a weight of about one ounce – half or a third of that required today. This lightness of action corresponded with the technique of the time, which was very different from the powerful and sometimes brutal attack of our own time. The first German pianists had naturally transferred to the piano the discreet touch inherited from the clavichord. It also facilitated the execution of those ornaments handed down to the piano in the literature of the harpsichord; but on the other hand it limited the degree of tonal colour available, which on the modern piano is so wide. From 1789 Stein replaced the *genouillères* with foot pedals; for the soft pedal he adopted Cristofori's ingenious system of the *una corda* (the keys being made to slip slightly to one side to strike only one of each pair of strings, thus producing a softer, and more subtle, sound).

In 1794, Stein's children, Maria Anna (Nanette) and Matthäus Andreas, seven years her junior, transferred the paternal workshop to Vienna. Nanette (1769-1833) was a striking personality, of wide accomplishments, a singer, a pianist, a woman of letters, who was to become one of Beethoven's most devoted friends in Vienna.[1]

Nanette became the wife of the Viennese piano maker, Johann Andreas Streicher (1761-1833), who, in his turn, perfected Stein's action. In 1823, the same year that Erard launched his double escapement action, Streicher produced his *Patent-Flügel*, in which, with the object of obtaining more force, the hammers strike from above the strings. As a result, the keyboard was placed above the level of the case itself. Later, however, he abandoned this arrangement. On the advice of Beethoven, who was a veritable punisher of pianos, Streicher applied himself to strengthening the construction of the piano and to increasing its volume, especially by means of a second soundboard.

Streicher's business was carried on by his son, Johann Baptiste Streicher (1796-1833). The firm had acquired world-wide fame, and its workshops produced an enormous number of instruments. The lightness of touch and the agreeable tone of these instruments assured Austrian supremacy in piano manufacture in German-speaking countries until the middle of the nineteenth century, after which Northern Germany became more important. Nevertheless, and in spite of its relative fragility and the special technique which this necessitates, the old Austrian action, perfected, of course, is still in use in its country of origin.

Until now we have only discussed the grand piano. Before con-

---

[1] When she was eight years old she had played for Mozart who, while criticising her touch, nevertheless found genius in her. In the last years of her life, Nanette gave up piano manufacture to devote herself entirely to literary work. It was she who translated into German the six volumes of Gall's *Anatomy and Physiology of the Nervous System.* An only son of Matthäus Stein, Karl Andreas (1797-1863) was also a piano builder, as well as a virtuoso on that instrument and a prolific composer.

tinuing we shall examine its rival, the square piano, which played a particularly important part in early English piano manufacture. Invented towards the middle of the eighteenth century the square piano (Italian, *piano a tavolo* or *tavolino*; German, *Tafel-Klavier*; French, *piano carré*) was to hold its own for close on a hundred years, concurrently with the grand and the upright piano. The square piano was the form under which the new instrument established itself in England before conquering France. But great and prolonged though its success was, it was only temporary. We shall follow its history until its disappearance towards the middle of the nineteenth century.

The form of the square piano was obviously derived from that of the clavichord and the virginal. The clavichord being particularly popular in Germany, it was not unnatural that Germany should give birth to its successor, the square piano. It was created in 1758 (hence about fifty years after the first grand piano) by Christian Ernst Friederici (1709-1780) of Gera in Saxony.[1] Friederici christened his invention with the bizarre name of *fortbien*, obviously a corruption of *fortepiano*. Thus we read in a list of objects having belonged to Mozart in the Mozart Museum at Salzburg the name 'forte-biano'.

As in the clavichord, the strings are at right angles to the keys, not parallel as in the grand piano. This no doubt permitted many clavichords to be transformed into 'squares' by the substitution of hammers for tangents. In the bass the strings are brass, wrapped with a metallic thread to increase their weight, consequently permitting them to be shorter than the long bass strings of the grand piano. This process had already been applied to the clavichord and had always remained in use.[2] At first the wrest-plank block was placed at the side of the case. The damper generally consisted of a cloth-covered rod.

The action of the square piano remained for a long time rudimentary. Its most typical form is the old English action which we shall discuss later on. By comparison with the contemporary grand pianos, the tone of early squares was thin, and in France the instrument justly received the sobriquet of the 'kettle'. Though it retained its essential faults, it was, nevertheless, continually improved up to the moment of its

---

[1] It is remarkable that Saxony, the birthplace of some of Germany's greatest musicians (Bach, Handel, Schumann and Wagner) was also the cradle of German piano building with Schröter, Silbermann, Stein and Friederici, as well as the seat of the oldest schools of instrument makers (at Markneukirchen, Klingenthal, etc. Friederici's brother, Christian Gottfried (1714-77) was also an organ builder of repute, and the latter's son Christian Gottlob (1750-1805) carried on his uncle's business.

[2] It will be recalled that the pitch of a string is determined by several factors: its length, its thickness, its tension and its material density.

26 Grand pianoforte by Anton Walter, Vienna, c 1785. Compass FF – g^3. FF
– a^1 bichord, b^1 – g^3 trichord. The case is of walnut, and stands on five
tapering legs; three knee-pedals (*genouillères*) control, respectively, a *piano*
stop, a 'bassoon' stop, and the dampers. Walter's reputation stood as high
as Stein's; he was a friend of Joseph Haydn, and made instruments for
Beethoven and, probably, Mozart (the music desk on this one is a copy of
that on the piano in Mozart's birthplace in Salzburg, believed to be by
Walter, though unsigned). *Kunsthistorisches Museum, Vienna.*

disappearance. The tone was improved, the keyboard extended to six octaves, the wooden frame was gradually strengthened by the addition of metal braces, until a complete iron frame was introduced by Petzold in 1829; in 1843 Pierre fitted it with the double escapement.

One of the most curious features in some early nineteenth-century pianos (in response to the detestable musical taste of the time) was their multiple pedals, by which there were produced different effects of timbre, intended especially for imitative pieces such as musical renderings of battles and storms. There were 'bassoon' pedals which lowered on to the strings a spiral of parchment or paper causing a pattering sound; a 'lute' pedal – indicated by the sign △ – which muted the strings by means of a strip of felt (similar to the 'buff' stop of the harpsichord, see page 37); a 'Turkish' pedal which sounded little bells, metallic rods, a side drum and a miniature bass drum.[1] These various stops were originally worked by hand registers, like the stops of the harpsichord, later by knee-pedals and finally by foot-pedals.

In Germany, where it was invented, the square piano's popularity spread rapidly. It inherited the confusing name of *klavier,* previously given to the organ and afterwards to the clavichord. 'The pianoforte,' wrote C. P. E. Bach, 'is built in two forms, the square and the grand. In the current language the first is the *klavier,* or properly speaking, the *pianoforte;* the second is known as the *flügel* (grand piano).' In Leipzig, Mozart tried in vain to buy from the *cantor* Doles a square piano which had won his heart. Nevertheless, C. P. E. Bach and other teachers recommended to pupils the grand piano – with its heavier action – to strengthen their fingers.

The success of the square piano was particularly great in England. With its more practicable shape and advantageous price, it easily rivalled the grand piano for domestic use. Towards 1800, small square pianos were sold in London for twenty-five guineas. The grand piano, though obviously a superior instrument, was limited more to the concert hall. Enormous numbers of square pianos were constructed. The instrument was even introduced into oriental harems, for which purpose it was mounted with short legs so that the pianist could sit on cushions placed on the floor. Many square pianos still survive in the attics of private houses or in old-fashioned drawing-rooms, where they are used as side-tables. Their owners, like many antique dealers, are regularly

[1] The strident, exotic qualities of Turkish military music, with its liberal use of percussion instruments, attracted the attention of European armies quite early in the eighteenth century, and it was not long before it acquired a vogue in serious music – as we can see from the fact that composers like Gluck, Haydn, Mozart and Beethoven all made use of such effects. (Ed.)

27 Grand pianoforte by Erard Frères, Paris, 1803 (No. 133). Compass FF - c⁴. Trichord. The case is of mahogany, and the front legs incorporate a rail with four pedals: *una corda*, sourdine, dampers, 'lute'. The firm of Erard presented the instrument to Beethoven in 1803, who used it for some fifteen years. *Kunsthistorisches Museum, Vienna.*

mistaken about the nature of these instruments which, because of their archaic appearance and sound, they habitually call 'harpsichords' or 'spinets'.

Some years before the appearance of the square piano, that is in 1745, Friederici had produced an instrument with a vertical case to replace the upright spinet or clavicytherium. This instrument was of pyramidal shape, and was the forerunner of our upright piano. In opposition to the name *fortbian* which Friederici gave to his square piano, he had called the pyramidal the *bienfort,* a name perhaps derived from the fact that the pyramidal piano required a powerful touch. Only two specimens of this instrument, with Friederici's mark, have been preserved, one in the Museum of the Brussels Conservatoire and the other in Goethe's house in Frankfurt.

The early vertical piano was simply a grand set on end, and took the form of a tall cupboard on legs; in later models the case went to the bottom of the instrument, the keyboard running across it at a convenient height and being connected to the action by a system of trackers. It was also sometimes built in 'giraffe' form, with the harp-shape of the soundboard extended to the case, and sometimes a 'lyre' shape in response to the rage for the antique shapes which was characteristic of the Empire style. This last form was a speciality of the builder Johann Christian Schleip of Tüngeda and later Berlin. The builder's imagination was given free rein in the extravagant ornamentation and the sumptuous luxury of these instruments, especially in those built during the Empire, with their marquetry, their bronze brackets, mother-of-pearl keys, statuettes, draperies, etc. But from the artistic point of view the results were mediocre, and these early vertical instruments were far from meeting with the success of the horizontal instruments, either square or grand. Since the strings were vertical to the keyboard, special mechanical difficulties arose.

It might seem logical to assume that the piano was introduced directly into France from Germany. On the contrary, it was from London that Paris received the new instrument. In 1770 in Paris, Virbès announced an audition of 'an instrument with hammers, like those in England'. The following year the first imported piano was lampooned as follows:

> Quoi, cher ami, tu me viens d'Angleterre?
> Hélas! comment peut-on lui déclarer la guerre?[1]

And from the vaudevillist, Piis:

> Avec un flegme anglais le piano se traîne.[2]

Still later the *Encyclopédie* (Technical Section) says: 'From Saxony the invention penetrated to London, from where practically all the pianos which are sold in France come to us'.

---

[1] What, my dear friend, you come to me from England?
Alas! How can we declare war on her?

[2] With an English phlegm the piano drags along.

86

28 Grand pianoforte by John Broadwood, London, 1806 (No. 3448). Compass
FF - c⁴. Trichord. The case is of mahogany and, with its trestle stand, is
visibly related to that of the classical English harpsichord, as built by such
makers as Shudi and Kirckman (see plates 16 and 17). Notice the elegant
brass fittings and the elaborate music desk, which is adjustable for both
angle and height. The left and centre pedals raise the dampers (the bass
and treble register being independent), the right shifts the keyboard to the
right, to strike two strings (*due corde*) or, if a stop inside the right cheek
is raised, one (*una corda*). *Private collection.*

Hence it was the English action instead of the German or Viennese
which was first employed in France. In 1780 de La Borde also stated that
most of the pianos sold in France were of English origin. Among the
instruments seized from the *émigrés* were half a dozen pianos by Schoene

29 Square pianoforte by Johann Christoph Zumpe, London, 1767. Compass
GG – f³, but without GG ♯ . Bichord. The case is of mahogany, as is
the trestle stand, and the instrument is very similar in appearance to a
clavichord (see plate 1). Two hand-stops inside the case, to the left of the
keyboard, raise and lower the dampers (the bass and treble registers being
independent). The instrument is typical of the early English 'square'
(really oblong) piano, and is the earliest known instrument of this kind
of normal disposition (one by Zumpe dated 1766 has divided accidentals
for tuning in unequal temperament). *Victoria and Albert Museum, London.*

of London. English manufacture was to maintain its prestige in France for
half a century. As late as 1827, to justify a prize awarded to a French piano,
the highest compliment was to call it 'equal to the best English pianos'. The
English industry had, moreover, remained particularly active, and was to
remain so until the last quarter of the nineteenth century. London had no
fewer than two hundred firms which either made or sold pianos, that is to
say, two-thirds again as many as Paris. We must therefore turn first to
English manufacture.

It was not unnaturally Germans who popularised the new instrument
in England and fostered its production. Johann Christian Bach
(1735-1782) J. S. Bach's youngest son, lived in London from 1762, where he
was the first to play the piano in public and where he gave piano lessons to

the Queen. At the same time his keyboard compositions were published for 'Harpsichord or Piano'. He was followed by Clementi who set up his establishment in London as pianist and teacher in 1770, and who published in London three years later some of the first compositions written expressly and exclusively for the pianoforte.

We have spoken of the Swiss Burkhard Tschudi or Shudi (1702-73) who settled in London as a builder of harpsichords. In 1763 he went into partnership with the Scotsman John Broadwood for the manufacture of pianos. But the real founder of the English industry, the creator of the primitive English action, was the German, Zumpe, one Silbermann's former workmen, who about 1760 established himself in London, where he later became 'the father of the commercial piano'. This was of course the square piano, which became the typical national piano, perhaps the more easily since it recalled in shape the English virginals.

The builder who worked most assiduously to perfect the square piano - and indeed the greatest English builder - was John Broadwood (1732-1812) who became Shudi's son-in-law. He made the case heavier and stronger and in 1788 moved the wrest-plank (in which the tuning pins are fixed) from the right side to the back of the case. From 1790 to 1794, Broadwood extended the keyboard to five and a half and finally to six octaves. The great builder was succeeded by his son James (1772-1851). From its foundation to the middle of the nineteenth century the firm constructed more than one hundred thousand instruments.

An improvement particularly important to the square piano, from which it passed to other models, consisted in arranging the strings in two superimposed planes, which economised space and reduced the dimensions of the instrument. It is difficult to say exactly who was the inventor of this fruitful device which has even been attributed to Hillebrand as far back as 1790. In her important work, The Piano-Forte, Rosamond Harding gathered much information on this subject, from which we may extract the following chronology.

It seems that Henri Pape of Paris was, in 1828, the originator of the system of cross-stringing. He was an ingenious German builder whom we shall speak of further on. In 1833, an American firm, Bridgeland & Jardine, exhibited in New York a piano in which the bass strings crossed over the treble. Meiszner followed suit the year after in Vienna. In 1835, Pierre-Frédéric Fischer patented the system in London, but cross-stringing had already been used the same year by Gerock of Cornhill, London, from a design by Theobald Boehm, the celebrated inventor of the 'Boehm' flute.

Finally, in 1847 the Belgian maker, Vogelsangs, took out a similar patent.

The so-called English grand action, which is still in use today – after countless improvements, of course – dates from about 1775. Created by a Dutchman, Americus Backers, with assistance from his apprentices' Robert Stodart and John Broadwood, it is once again Zumpe's action, but supplied with an improved version of Cristofori's damper.[1] Stronger but heavier than the Italian piano, the primitive English piano differed from the Viennese in that, with bigger strings requiring heavier hammers, it demanded a more vigorous touch. It produced a strong and prolonged tone, but inclined to be dull and lacking in brilliance in the treble and coarse in the bass. The deep fall of the hammer made rapid passages hard to play, a serious fault inasmuch as the first piano literature had inherited, especially in the work of J. C. Bach, the ornaments of the harpsichord style. The Viennese action, on the other hand, by its lightness and ease of play, favoured rapid and brilliant passages and encouraged composers to write them.[2]

The first piano virtuosos in Paris were two Germans who lived there, Johann Schobert (1720-67), a forerunner of Mozart as a composer of piano concertos, and Johann Eckardt (1735-1809). According to de Bricqueville (in *The Harpsichord of Madame du Barry and the Piano of Marie-Antoinette*) the piano is supposed to have first appeared in Paris in 1759. In 1768, Mademoiselle Lechantre played the piano for the first time at the 'Concert spirituel', not, however, with marked success. But in 1775, the celebrated singer, Albanese, declared that he preferred the piano to the harpsichord for the accompaniment of singing, because 'it is more round in tone and consequently more like the human voice'. In 1771, the son of Virbès – whom we have mentioned – 'had the honour to play the *fortepiano* before Madame la Dauphine'. And a few years later, among the instruments seized from the *émigrés,* there were no fewer than fifty-five pianos. A literature began to grow up around the new instrument, but – as in London and elsewhere – the older

[1] A grand piano of 1772 by Backers is in the Russell Collection in Edinburgh, and another of 1775 is in the Benton Fletcher Collection in Fenton House, Hampstead, London. (Ed.)

[2] Such was the case with Hummel (1778-1837) a pupil of Mozart's and a brilliant pianist, whose compositions abound in ornaments and betray the influence of the Viennese instruments. At the end of his *Pianoforte Method* (1827) he writes: "The German action can be played easily by the most delicate fingers. It sounds clearly and promptly. . . . As for instruments with the English action it is fair to say that they are solidly built and produce a great volume of sound, but they are not so "voluble" as the German pianos, since the touch is heavier and, the keys going down further, a certain time is required for the escapement when one wishes to repeat a note.' We may add to Hummel's remarks the fact that the Viennese action, simpler than the English, was also more durable, easier to repair and less expensive.

harpsichord was not neglected. Edelmann published duos, J. P. Trapay a 'symphonie concertante' for harpsichord and piano. In 1771 Mademoiselle Branche composed 'Ariettes' for harpsichord or piano, and Romain Brasseur three sonatas with the same indication.

We have said that the first pianos played in France were of English importation. To these must be added German instruments, especially those of Johann Heinrich Silbermann, whose instruments (at least according to Gerber in his *Lexikon der Tonkünstler*) were the best to be found in Paris. The origin of French piano manufacture is obscure. We have noted the initiative of Virbès in 1770. In the same year we find an instrument marked: *Johannes Kilianus Mercken, Parisiis,* 1770. Afterwards came Erard (1777), Hildebrandt and Hoffman (1783), and Duvernier (1784).

We should like especially to emphasise the part played in this movement by the celbrated Belgian harpsichord maker Pascal Taskin, because it seems to be unknown even to the best historians.[1] Now Taskin, according to Becdelièvre in his *Biographie liégeoise,* constructed his first piano in 1776, in other words a year before Erard. Erard restricted himself at first to the square piano; his earliest grand dates from 1797, at least ten years after those of Taskin, Taskin's surviving pianos are, like his harpsichords, extremely rare, and he can only have made very few. Not one is mentioned in the *Annonces et avis divers* of the time. In one of his letters – in which, incidentally, he betrays himself as an illiterate – he writes: 'Madame Victoire, the Queen's Aunt, has bought one from me for 4,000 francs . . . . Doubtless the Queen . . . could not afford one because of present circumstances which are so disquieting.'[2] Among the instruments seized from the *émigrés* there was a 'fortepiano in the shape of a harpsichord' (in other words, a grand piano) by Taskin.

If today Taskin's harpsichords are rare, his pianos are even rarer. Three only have been found, one a square piano which formerly belonged to Eugène de Bricqueville in Paris, another which belonged to Marie-Antoinette in the Museum at Versailles, and finally, the one which is in the Schloss Charlottenburg in Berlin. We should like to dwell for an instant on this last instrument. It is a luxurious example in a mahogany case, richly inlaid with rare woods, the fluting and capitals of the

---

[1] See, for instance, the works of Fischhof, Rimbault, Ponsicchi, Pierre, Chouquet, Hipkins, Blondel and moreover most of the biographies of Taskin!

[2] 'Madame Victoire tente du Roi men a acheté un 4000. . . . On ne se doutterois pas que la Reine en ayant été pour ainsi dire entousiasmé se soit privé d'en acheter un, cela sandoute relativement à la circonstance du temps, qui ne laisse pas de nous inquiéter.

legs of solid brass, etc. Its most remarkable feature is the stringing. Instead of each note having two strings tuned in unison, as is normal, a single string of double length is used. The string is doubled over the hitch-pin, and held by a screw which can be turned to regulate the tension.

Taskin seems to have been the inventor of this system, especially praised by the *Encyclopédie*, a system which has been patented and tried several times since, notably by Pleyel in 1826, in his *unicorde*. While Boisselot in 1839 applied the same principle to his *clédiharmonique*, it was to Taskin that the critics referred. On the other hand, Taskin's action is crude. He seems to have been unaware of escapement mechanism which, seventy years after Cristofori, and in such a city as Paris, is astonishing. The key, when depressed, raises a lever which moves a jack fixed to a leather-covered hammer which it throws against the string. Simultaneously, the damper, fixed obliquely to the shank of the hammer, rises from the string, allowing it to vibrate (see Appendix, Figure 12).

In 1788 Taskin's piano was the object of a very favourable report drawn up by three delegates of the Academy of Sciences, published in the *Annals* of the Academy, reproduced in the *Avant-Coureur* the following year, and, in part, in the *Encyclopédie*. It was praised the year after that in an article in the *Mercure de France*, which was republished by the *Musikalisches Wochenblatt* and soon afterwards in Gerber's *Lexikon der Tonkünstler*. But all this publicity came to nothing. The pioneers of the piano were indeed unlucky. Taskin, like Cristofori, Marius and Schröter, got nothing out of his invention. A late-comer to piano building who vanished obscurely in the turmoil of the Revolution, the Walloon builder had no time to profit by his new instrument. This success was reserved for Sébastien Erard, thirty years his junior, the genius who invented the double escapement mechanism.

Before continuing it might be as well to point out the imperfections and the fragility of the pianos with which for many years the great masters of music had to content themselves, deficiencies which made the use of these instruments hazardous and almost an adventure. The clavichord, with its simple mechanism, had quickly reached its perfection. Because of its complexity, the piano arrived much more slowly. Contemporaries have left us some astonishing testimonials of these early difficulties. Here are a few lines on the subject from the memoirs of the Bohemian-born composer Antonín Reicha (1770-1836), who became one of the most eminent theoreticians of French musical composition in the beginning of the nineteenth century, and from whom César Franck received lessons. In Bonn, Reicha had struck up a friendship

92

with the young Beethoven whom he later met in Vienna, and about whom the following passage is written:

'One day', Reicha records, 'Beethoven played at Court a concerto of Mozart's and he asked me to turn the pages for him. All the time the strings of the instrument kept snapping and jumping into the air, while the hammers got entangled in the broken strings. Beethoven, wishing to finish the piece at all costs, begged me to disengage the hammers and remove the broken strings whenever he paused in playing. My job was harder than his, for I had constantly to jump to the right, to the left, to run around the piano to get at all the hammers.'

In 1812, the Viennese publisher Gözzl, relating an occasion when Beethoven was improvising on the piano added, in the most natural way in the world: 'It was no longer a question of making music since half the strings had snapped'. This situation, only improving by degrees, was to last for a long time still.[1] Receiving a visit from Johann Stumpff, a London harp maker, in 1824 Beethoven complained to him about the faults of the contemporary piano 'on which one can play nothing with force and effect'. He showed Stumpff the instrument he had received from Broadwood. 'What a spectacle offered itself to my view!' wrote the harp maker. 'There was no sound left in the treble and broken strings were mixed up like a thorn bush after a gale.' In this same year 1824, the young Liszt, playing for the first time in Paris, had to stop several times so that a string might be re-tuned or a broken one replaced.

The Viennese school was notable above all for the improvements it brought to the primitive instruments of Cristofori and Silbermann; but it remained to English and French builders to bring about new progress. The inventor of the modern piano was Sébastien Erard.

---

[1] Beethoven owned a whole series of pianos. At the very beginning of his career his friend and patron, Count Waldstein, had presented him with an instrument built by the old German builder, Tufenbruch, which the composer piously kept all his life. It was a miniature piano, easy to carry, enclosed in a long flat box, fitted with a music stand, pen and ink and candlesticks.

The first piano Beethoven owned in Vienna was made by the builder Vogel of Budapest, and had been given to him by the Princess Lichnowsky. About 1800 he had one signed Yakesch. Afterwards he showed a marked predilection for the instruments of Stein-Streicher. In 1803 he received as a mark of homage an Erard, now in Vienna (see plate 27). In 1816, Streicher built him at his own request a piano with a keyboard of six and a half octaves. In 1818, Broadwood of London sent the master an instrument which, in spite of the composer's affection for Nanette Streicher, aroused his enthusiasm. Finally in 1823, Beethoven had a piano by Conrad Graf of Vienna (now in the house of his birth at Bonn) fitted with quadruple stringing, in an attempt to enable the composer to hear it.

It is interesting to follow in Beethoven's sonatas the growing range of these instruments. The following examples will illustrate the point.

I. Notes lacking in the bass:
Op. 2, No. 3, first movement, final bars of the exposition:

The semiquaver pattern should be obviously be continued to
the end.

Op. 10, No. 3, first bars:

The whole passage should be in octaves.

II. Notes lacking in the treble:
Op. 10, No. 3, bars 21-2:

The final high F sharp is lacking.

A little further on:

The first figure, including the octave leap, should obviously continue to the end.

Op. 14, No. 2, first movement, bar 102:

apparently for

according to the musical context.

Sébastien Erard, in reality Ehrhard, born in Strasbourg in 1752, arrived in 1768 in Paris, where he died in 1831. Starting as a workman in the workshop of an obscure maker of harpsichords, he soon established himself on his own account, and from the harpsichord passed to the pianoforte. It was on the orders of the Maréchale de Villeroy, who installed him in a workshop in her château, that Erard constructed his first piano in 1777.

Like the Belgian Adolphe Sax some years later, Erard aroused the enmity of his rivals, who accused him of working outside the corporation without a licence. But the King, who protected the builder, granted him a licence on his own authority. As soon as his reputation was established, Erard brought his brother Jean-Baptiste to Paris to join him. They started by building small square pianos with double strings and five octaves. Sébastien Erard then built for Marie-Antoinette an instrument with two keyboards, an organ and piano combined. His talent, backed by royal favour, brought him instant celebrity. Among the seized *émigré* instruments his trademark was the commonest. On the outbreak of the French Revolution the Erard brothers retired to London, and it was in London that Sébastien patented his first grand piano. In 1796 he returned to Paris, leaving the direction of the London branch of the firm to his nephew Pierre, who was also to distinguish himself by many inventions. We find Sébastien Erard in London again between 1808 and 1815.

Though, as we believe, Taskin built grand pianos in Paris before Erard did, Erard's products were far more advanced than Taskin's. In particular, the system which Erard brought back from London, and which he first applied in Paris in 1797, represented a happy combination of his personal experience and of his study of English manufacture. One improvement followed another.

We are told that it was Erard who first substituted wrapped steel

Op. 110, first movement, bar 75:

The ascending pattern should continue to the end.
For this last work Beethoven had a Broadwood piano with six octaves, but the extension was in the bass, not the treble.

The passages cited above, with others of the same sort, have generally been re-edited in modern editions according to the probable intentions of the composer.

strings in the bass notes for the brass strings which had been used until then. He extended the range of the keyboard to five and a half octaves. For the soft pedal he used a band of felt which came between the hammers and the strings. He invented the agraffes fixing the strings to the wrest-pin block bridge.[1] He created a new system of dampers called 'bayonnette' from the shape. He made the case heavier and reinforced it by an iron bar above the strings. We have already seen that he was the first in Paris to replace knee-pedals by foot-pedals, in imitation of Broadwood.

But his chief contribution was to the perfection of the action itself. He had combined the English action, introduced by him into Paris, with the innovations of the great Viennese builders, combining the solidity of the former with the agreeable touch, quickness of response, and sweetness of sound of the latter. This he had done largely on the advice of the Czech composer Dussek, who had settled in Paris in 1808 as Talleyrand's Chapel Master, and who was used to the lightness of the Austrian pianos. In 1795, Erard achieved his first notable improvement, an escapement mechanism derived from Cristofori's principle, with the jack, detached from the key, freeing the hammer from the key's control and letting it fall back quickly after its action, ready to strike again. (See Appendix, Figure 13.) This mechanism was later named the 'simple escapement' and was perfected by Erard by 1816. Its disadvantage still consisted in the length of the curve twice described (going and returning) by the hammer, preventing the rapid repetition of a note.

But finally, in 1822, after many experiments and trials going back as far as 1809, Erard put the seal on his life's work with his famous double escapement mechanism, which was launched at the Exposition of 1823. To the double escapement mechanism, an invention of genius and this time entirely Erard's own, we owe the suppleness and sensitivity of the modern piano. With double escapement, the hammer, caught by the second escapement, hesitates, as it were, to fall back completely and gives the first escapement time to re-establish its striking position. Thus the key can again act upon the hammer and, at any point of the hammer's course, throw it against the string. The result is a capacity for quick repetition unknown with the old system. Also, with the old system, a repeated note, especially in the *tremolo* and the trill, could only be played *forte*; with a soft touch the length of the hammer's fall took too much time. Double escapement avoids this fault.

[1] The agraffes are the brass studs pierced by as many holes as there are unison strings to the note which act as a 'nut' for the particular note. The wrest-pin block bridge is the pinned rail with its bed of wood or iron where the wrest-pins or tuning pegs are fixed.

96

In spite of its evident advantages, the new mechanism had its adversaries who pointed out how quickly the complicated arrangement – which was in truth rather fragile – would wear out. Pleyel, for instance, remained obstinately attached to the simple escapement. But the striking superiority of the new system, praised by Thalberg and other virtuosos, rapidly overcame this opposition, and double escapement was adopted everywhere. Erard himself continued to improve it. Others, like Pleyel, Kriegelstein and Blüthner, invented their own ingenious applications of the same principle.[1]

We may note here the singular importance of the part played by the Germans in the popularisation of the piano and the creation of the piano industry in France as in other countries. If the construction of stringed instruments was a skill chiefly of Italian and French origin (Germany only possessing the Tyrolean School of *luthiers*, directly derived from the Italian), and if Germany was not rich in great violin makers, piano building seems to be peculiarly fitted to her industrial genius. Italy had dropped Cristofori's invention; it was the Germans who developed it and introduced the new instrument into international musical life. We have noted their contributions in England. In Paris, as we have seen, the two principal piano virtuosos were both Germans. We have observed the success in Paris of the pianos of Johann Heinrich Silbermann (1727-99), a nephew of Gottfried, who was established in Strasbourg, and we have seen that the Erards were from Strasbourg. Kriegelstein was also an Alsatian, a native of Riquewihr; Herz – at the same time composer, virtuoso and builder whose firm had an immediate success – was Viennese. Freudenthaler, one of the oldest Parisian builders, maker of more than two thousand instruments, who supplied the Opéra and the Italian Theatre, was from Neckargartach near Heilbronn. Other makers of German origin were Hillebrand, Klein, Schwörr, Wölfel, Roller, Pfeiffer, whose square pianos were particularly prized, and his contemporary associate, William Petzold (to whom Fétis ascribes many improvements to the square piano), Schwander of Lauterbach and his successor Herrburger of Dauendorf, whose firm before the first world war made nearly one hundred thousand mechanisms a year. And finally, there were Pape and Pleyel.

[1] We may recall that well before his double escapement for the piano Erard had already created his 'double movement harp', eliminating half the pedals of the old model and giving the harp its standard form still in use. It is not too much to imagine a kind of connection between these two great inventions, the one having perhaps inspired the other. Finally Erard was also a skilful organ builder. The organ in the chapel of the Tuileries came from his workshop.
A daughter of Sébastien Erard became the wife of Spontini, the composer.

Henri Pape (born in Sarstedt near Hanover in 1789), was an interesting figure. He arrived in Paris in 1811, where he first worked in Pleyel's workshop, afterwards setting up for himself. He began by making square pianos with English actions, afterwards turning his attention to grand pianos. An inventive genius of the Adolphe Sax type, Pape patented no fewer than a hundred and thirty-seven inventions, all for the piano. Most of them have been forgotten, but one of them – of capital importance – has been internationally accepted: the felting of hammers. Up until his time, the head of the hammer had been covered either in sheepskin or buckskin as in Vienna, which gave a hard, dry tone, or else in flannel or a mixture of wool and cotton as in London (where even a sponge hammer had been tried). It was Pape who, in 1826, created the felt hammer, universally adopted since.[1]

In 1839, four years after Boehm in London, Pape introduced into Paris the arrangement of cross-stringing. He also patented the idea, already old, but never very successful, of the hammer striking the string from above. To him we also owe a 'piano-console' (1828), a charming instrument, something between a square and an upright, less cumbersome than the square, the case coming no higher than the keyboard. He even built a circular piano (1834), constructed on a hemisphere in copper, like a kettle drum. Finally, by reducing the case of the ordinary piano, its metal parts, etc., he succeeded in lessening the weight of the instrument by about two hundred pounds; although at the same time he made enormous pianos called 'sarcophaguses' for export to America.

Pape's name today is unjustly forgotten. The fate of Pleyel's name was quite the opposite. Pleyel became Erard's most redoubtable competitor. Born in Ruppersthal in Lower Austria in 1757 (the twenty-fourth of thirty-eight children) Ignace Pleyel died in Paris in 1831. A composer and publisher of music, he founded his piano-building firm in Paris in 1807. Subsidised by Méhul, the firm rapidly acquired a considerable importance. Dussek, Steibelt and Thalberg as pianists had made the reputation of Erard's instruments. Pleyel's pianos, together with those of Pape, were the instruments preferred by Moscheles, Kalkbrenner (who was associated with Pleyel's business) Cramer and John Field. When Ignace Pleyel died, the directorship of the firm passed to his son Camille (1788-1855), and it was then that it received its final hall-mark of fame from a virtuoso younger and greater

[1] The material forming the head of the hammer has a considerable effect upon the tone produced. Even the quality of the felt, the length of its fibres and their weave play an important part. Nowadays the felting of hammers is submitted to a process of pricking by tiny needles to improve its elasticity.

than any of his predecessors. Frédéric Chopin chose the Pleyel piano as peculiarly fitted for his 'singing' technique, as giving him 'his own proper tone', other instruments yielding only a 'ready-made tone'. It was also with Pleyel instruments that Liszt and Rubinstein made their Paris débuts. The two rival houses of Pleyel and Erard prospered side by side; by the end of the nineteenth century each had built its 100,000th instrument.[1]

In the nineteenth century French piano makers continued to multiply. Statistics gathered in 1847 reveal the existence in Paris alone of 197 makers, a figure which includes keyboard and case makers.[2] The price of concert model grand pianos ranged from 3,500 to 4,000 francs; for smaller models, from 2,000 to 2,500; for uprights and squares from 1,200 to 2,500 francs (there were twenty-five francs to the pound sterling). In the second half of the nineteenth century the number of makers dwindled considerably. In France it dropped by two-thirds. Not that the number of instruments built fell off, but the industry was concentrated more and more in the great houses, small firms disappearing one after the other, in conformity with the general law of industrial evolution.

The most famous British builder, for a long while, remained John Broadwood, whose firm, transformed into a limited liability company, still exists, and whose workshops rarely employed fewer than 600 craftsmen. We have seen that Beethoven played one of his pianos. From 1808 to 1818, James Shudi Broadwood, son and successor to John, began to use iron braces for supporting the strain imposed by the stringing, a system taken up by Erard in 1822.

Another well-known English make was that of Longman & Broderip, a firm founded in 1767 by William Collard, with which Clementi was later associated. Muzio Clementi, the eminent Italian composer, was, like Henri Herz in Paris, a composer, virtuoso and builder at the same time; some years before his death, he relinquished the direction of the firm to Collard. It was also in England that Allen and James Thom built, in 1820, the first iron frame in assembled parts, while Stodart invented a framework of tubular metal. Shortly after the middle of the

[1] The parallel between the two firms extended to a curious coincidence, pointed out by C. Pierre. Sébastien Erard and Ignace Pleyel died in the same year, 1831, and their respective successors, Pierre Erard and Camille Pleyel, also both died the same year, 1855.

[2] As in the other domains of national activity – including musical life itself – French instrumental manufacture is especially concentrated in Paris. We may note, however, in the provinces the firms of Mangeot in Nancy, and the Boisselot Brothers in Marseilles. In Germany, on the contrary, a country of decentralisation, the industry is distributed throughout the nation, with a certain predominance in Saxony.

30 Square pianoforte by Longman and Broderip, London, *c* 1800. Compass FF – c⁴. Bichord. The case is of mahogany, with painted floral decorations on the name-board, as is the elegant stand on which the instrument rests. The pedal (a modern replacement) raises the dampers. *Private collection.*

nineteenth century, English manufacture had developed to such an extent that it could be considered the foremost in the world, but it has since declined from that position. This is partly due to the importance of the German industry which competed with English firms on their own territory and which, at the end of the nineteenth century, exported 20,000 pianos to Britain a year. To the names of the English builders we have already mentioned, we must limit ourselves to adding those of John Brinsmead, Chappell and Hopkinson.

From all that has gone before we have seen the importance, from the very beginning of the industry, of German piano manufacture. We have seen the immigrant German builders were very numerous in England, France and America. The same thing happened in every country, especially in Belgium and Russia. Naturally they also abounded in Germany itself, where in 1910 there were 300 piano factories, a number of which had been in existence for more than a century. To the names of the older makers to whom we have already referred we must add those of

Anton Walter of Vienna (see plate 26), much admired by Mozart, who owned one of his instruments, Christian Gottlob Hubert of Ansbach (1714-1793), Franz Jacob Späth or Spath of Ratisbon (c. 1714-1786, Mozart's favourite maker before he discovered Stein), Schiedmayer of Erlangen (1781), Ibach of Barmen (1794), Bösendorfer of Vienna (1828) and Blüthner of Leipzig (1853).

European manufacture was quickly followed by that of the new world, particularly concentrated in the United States, where its development was to become enormous, especially upon the arrival of numerous Germans. According to Alfred Dolge, writing in 1911, twenty-two contemporary American firms were of German origin. American manufacture was derived from both British and German industry. In 1775, in Philadelphia, Johann Behrend built the first American square piano. The square type of instrument, abandoned by European builders before the middle of the nineteenth century, enjoyed a much longer popularity in the United States. The heavier and more cumbersome grand piano at first found little favour, and European virtuosos visiting the United States brought their own instruments with them. Nor did the upright piano immediately catch on. The square remained the general favourite. Until the middle of the nineteenth century, almost every instrument constructed in the United States was of the square type. In 1880 they were still being made. Krakauer of New York introduced (though without success) huge squares seven feet long and supplied with every refinement. Steinway built a similar model with a seven-octave keyboard. Twenty years later the number of square pianos in circulation still weighed so heavily on the national industry that American piano manufacturers resolved to finish with them. At their congress in Atlantic City in 1903, they acquired, at the price of some hundreds of thousands of dollars, an enormous number of these instruments with which they erected, on the heights of Chelsea, a pyramid fifty feet high and set fire to it.

Although it was founded largely by foreigners, American piano manufacture nevertheless assumed its own special characteristics, aided by the fact that imported instruments stood up to the climate badly. In conformity with the national genius, the ingenuity of the national builders concentrated especially upon the reinforcement of the various parts of the instrument, and the extension of the metallic parts, a development favoured by the excellent quality of American iron and the advanced state of the local metallurgical industry. The frame was reinforced by iron supports, by parallel metal tubing and sheets, by iron braces over the strings. In 1825, Alpheus Babcock of Boston (imitated the following year by Pape and by Pleyel), patented a one-piece, cast-iron frame to which he added, five years later, Pape's system of cross-stringing, thus creating the prototype of the modern American piano. The rigidity of the iron frame, however, decreased the resonance of the strings, and the disadvantage was only overcome by increasing the size of the strings. In the improved version, the new iron-frame piano made a sensation at the World Exhibitions in Paris in 1862 and 1867. At the first of these Exhibitions, the pianos exhibited by Chickering, which represented the new type, obtained the first prize, the maker was given the *Légion d'honneur*, and shortly afterwards, the one-piece metallic frame was universally adopted. For cast iron Pleyel substituted forged iron and rolled steel as being lighter and stronger.

But the most famous of American piano manufacturers was to be Heinrich Steinweg (who was born in Wolfshage in the Harz Mountains in 1797 and died in New York in 1871). After beginning his career in Brunswick as an instrument maker, then as an organ builder, Steinweg decided to build pianos, constructing his first instrument in 1835 in Seesen, Harz. The political disturbances of 1848 having brought business to a stop, Steinweg sent his son Karl to America to try out the territory. The result of this inquiry was favourable and Steinweg embarked for America in 1850 with his sons Karl, Heinrich, Wilhelm and Albert, leaving his son Theodor as the chief of his business in Brunswick. In 1858 Theodor was joined by Friedrich Grotrian and the firm subsequently became known as Grotrian-Steinweg. Meanwhile, Heinrich Steinweg and his four other sons settled in New York, working with local manufacturers in order to study the methods of American piano making. In 1853, anglicising their name, they founded the firm of Steinway and Sons. Its prosperity was as extraordinary as it was rapid. Steinway and his sons had naturally begun with square pianos which they were soon making at the rate of fifty a week. But they wasted little time with this superannuated type, and quickly turned to the concert grand which they enriched with improvements which we shall discuss below.

Besides Steinway, there was also the firm of Baldwin, Mason and Hamlin, and more especially that of Chickering and Sons, of Boston and New York, the oldest native firm, founded in 1823 by Jonas Chickering (1798-1853). We have already mentioned the success gained by Chickering pianos at the Paris Exhibition. In brilliance and sonority they rivalled the Steinway instruments. The American piano, originally a mere offshoot of the European industry, soon influenced its parent, thanks to the skill and spirit of initiative shown by its makers.

31　Upright grand pianoforte by Clementi & Co., 1816. Compass FF – c⁴.
Trichord. This is a comparatively rare example of a true upright grand
piano, *i.e.* with the keyboard and action at the bottom of the instrument,
rather than mid-way across it as in some contemporary instruments and all
later 'uprights'. *Colt Clavier Collection, Bethersden, Kent.*

103

From all the above we can see that, from its origins until the middle of the nineteenth century, the piano building industry was concentrated chiefly in three countries, Germany, England and France, later joined by the United States. As the popularity of the instrument increased, the number of builders in every country rose, the three countries named maintaining the general direction of the industry. In recent years there has been a remarkable growth in the Japanese piano industry.

We can picture the importance thus acquired by an industry getting its raw materials – wood, metal, felt, ivory – from all parts of the world. This vast production – momentarily slowed down by the success of the radio, whose rise occurred at the same time as the world-wide economic crisis of 1930-3 – may be explained by the relative quickness with which the powerful instruments wear out. The piano is indeed short-lived when compared with the fragile violin, made of a few thin boards which tend to improve rather than deteriorate with age.

⸜In Belgium, the piano was played for the first time in Liège in 1769 by Jean Noël Hamal, chapel master and creator of the comic opera in Liège dialect (1709-1778). The industry soon became established in the country without however ever achieving the importance of the great international firms. This was not because of any technical inferiority of Belgian makers, but was rather due to economic factors, especially the unfavourable export situation artificially maintained by prohibitive tariffs. It was a long time ago when the last of the Belgian harpsichord makers, alarmed by the influx of foreign instruments, obtained from the Austrian government the imposition of the formidable tariff of 130 florins for each foreign instrument entering Belgium. There can be little doubt that this strangulation of trade and competition accounted for the fact that Belgian makers (with the exception of the German, P. Bull of Antwerp) limited themselves for a long while to the square piano, and then to the upright.

But Belgian makers were, nevertheless, numerous and active. At the World Exhibition of 1878, in Paris, the Belgian corporation was represented by ten builders, the most numerous after the English, who had eleven representatives (incidentally, the official report mentions every instrument except the Belgian ones).

The Belgian harpsichord industry was centred in Antwerp; the piano industry in Brussels. In 1830, twelve of the twenty-five Belgian makers worked in Brussels. One of the oldest of these was Henry van Casteel, who was working about 1775, followed by Winands, Adrien, the Daniel brothers, Ermel, Grœtaers and Hœberechts. Two particularly interesting figures towards the middle of the nineteenth century were H.

Lichtenthal and F. J. Vogelsangs – the first responsible for numerous technical innovations (he moved to St Petersburg in 1851), and the second the Belgian founder of the cross-stringing system; C. J. Sax, father of the inventor of the saxophone, a maker of wind instruments, also built pianos for which he took out many patents. The founders of the industry in Ghent appear to have been Symphorien Ermel and Dammekens. In Mons the builders included Eugène and Philippe Ermel, whose instruments 'were as good as the best forte-pianos coming from England' (according to a certificate dated 1785), and Louis Fétis – an uncle of the illustrious musicologist who, for reasons unknown to us, abstained from listing his relative in his *Biographie universelle des musiciens*. Finally, at Namur, a certain Frin patented in 1833 the first Belgian piano with an iron frame.

So far we have discussed only the grand piano, the square piano and the 'giraffe' and 'pyramidal' pianos. We must go back slightly in order to sketch in the history of the upright piano (Italian, *pianino*; German, *cabinet-pianoforte* and afterwards *aufrechtes klavier*; French, *piano droit*), which replaced the square, 'giraffe' and 'pyramidal' pianos as domestic instruments, just as the last two had in their day succeeded the *clavicitherium*.

The arrangement of the upright piano as we know it today is in one sense the reverse of the 'giraffe' and the 'pyramidal' in as much as the wrest-pin block (containing the tuning pins) is on top, while the stringing tapers off towards the bottom. An upright piano is called 'vertical', 'oblique' or 'half oblique', according to the arrangement of its strings. The action is either over-damper or under-damper, the former having dampers which act above the striking hammers, the latter having dampers which act below the hammers. Under-damper action is considered preferable (see Appendix, Figure 15). It must be admitted at once that in principle the upright piano can only be inferior to the grand piano, which has a more natural arrangement of strings and action. Nevertheless, the upright was to triumph, thanks to its relative cheapness, convenient shape and smaller size.

As we have pointed out in discussing the older types of upright instruments, the essential vice of the upright piano arises from its vertical mechanism. Already in 1811, the Viennese maker Bleyer, cited by Sachs, had written on this subject: 'When we examine this action closely, we observe the drops of sweat shed by its inventor'. With the upright the double escapement mechanism will not work by the simple laws of gravity as it does with the horizontally hinged hammer of the grand. It must be helped along by artificial means, in particular by

105

32　Grand pianoforte by Conrad Graf, Vienna, 1839 (No 2616). Compass CC
– g⁴, CC – FF# bichord, GG – g⁴ trichord. The case is of rosewood, and
the shape of the instrument, apart from the square cheeks and tail, is
already very close to that of the modern grand. The four pedals operate,
respectively, the *una corda*, two degrees of 'sourdine' (effected by cloth
strips of different thickness), and the dampers. Graf (who made a grand
piano for Beethoven in 1823) presented this instrument to Clara Wieck
on her marriage to Robert Schumann in 1840, and after Schumann's death
it passed to Brahms, who kept it until 1873. *Kunsthistorisches Museum,
Vienna.*

springs, the resistance of which naturally diminishes the crispness of the 'attack'. This results in a return to simple escapement, already described. Hence the quick repetition of a note becomes more difficult than with a grand piano. Great efforts have been made to remedy the faults inherent in the upright piano, efforts partly crowned with success when we consider the buzzing tone of the older instruments of this type. Nevertheless, the upright remains and must continue to remain inferior to the grand both in tone and in volume. This lack of volume is the result not only of its shorter strings, but also of the fact that the closed back of its case, normally set against a wall, muffles the sound, and finally because of the size and shape of the soundboard which in upright pianos is square instead of rounded as in the grand pianos.

We do not know for certain where or when the upright piano was invented. The invention has been attributed to Johann Schmitt of Salzburg in 1780, but without substantiation. A model of the same type is said to have been patented in England in 1798 by the Englishman, Robert Wornum. Lacking more ample evidence, however, the invention of the modern domestic upright piano must be credited to J. I. Hawkins, an English engineer resident in Philadelphia who, in 1800, patented the new instrument, supplied with an iron frame, under the name of the 'portable grand'.

In 1807, William Southwell of London (formerly of Dublin) built an upright in which the case rested on the ground. Considerable progress was made, again in England, by Robert Wornum with his *piccolo* piano, the action of which, greatly improved, became the international prototype, was taken up in Paris and became known as the 'English action'. In the *Encyclopédie Méthodique* of 1818, de Momigny stated that up until then only the English – particularly the firm of Clementi-Collard – had been seriously occupied with the upright piano. In Paris in 1827, an upright only three feet high, by Roller and Blanchet, allegedly based on an idea by one of Erard's craftsmen named Buller, excited lively interest. But the upright was popularised in Paris chiefly by Pape and Pleyel from 1839 onwards.

Until this time the upright was still rare in Germany, where it was falsely believed to be a French invention. Today its construction is universal.

We have now entered the modern period in the history of the piano, which may be said to have begun about the middle of the nineteenth century. From this moment, novelties and innovations from all countries are more and more frequent, and the instrument has been improved with a disconcerting rapidity. We can say that the modern piano, the piano we now play and listen to, scarcely goes back to the beginning of the present century. It is already a very different instrument from those which the great virtuosos of yesterday had at their disposal, especially from the point of view of volume and richness of tone. The *ff* of yesterday would hardly be as loud as the *mf* of today. Chopin's Pleyel piano had little in common with its present-day descendants. It would be fatiguing, and practically impossible, to enter into the details of the innovations which mark out this road towards the ideal keyboard instrument, innovations essentially technical, protected by thousands of patents, of which the majority are already forgotten and which were often mere repetitions of each other except in some minor detail intended to justify the patent. This fever of invention was excited (as it was in other branches of industry) by the ever growing number of world fairs where, at large expense, rival firms confronted each other with their auditions, prospectuses and testimonials calculated to overwhelm the visitor.[1] We shall limit ourselves to general remarks, beginning with the structure of the modern piano.

Before the use of cast iron, the framework of the piano was made of wood, strengthened by cross-beams. It is this framework which, in the last analysis, must support the immense tension of the strings. After the invention of iron frames, the woodwork could be much lighter in proportion to the solidity and the weight of the metal work which, in the modern piano, bears the entire tension of the strings. At the end of the frame is fixed the wrest-pin block, a strong piece of beechwood reinforced by laminations of about a quarter of an inch in thickness, into which are embedded the wrest-pins by which the strings are tightened and tuned. Beyond the wrest-pin block on the periphery of the frame the soundboard is fixed. The soundboard, like the belly of a violin, is designed to amplify the volume of the strings. It is a sheet of wood (generally Swiss pine) about three-eighths of an inch thick, gently arched and reinforced – like the belly of a violin – by spruce struts across the grain, which bind together the pieces making up the soundboard, and maintain its curvature. To the soundboard is glued the bridge over which the strings pass and which – again like the bridge of a violin – transmits the vibrations of the strings to the soundboard.

The strings, formerly of steel, and brass, are today of cold drawn steel.

[1] Oscar Paul relates that at the Universal Exhibition in Paris in 1867, Steinway and Chickering each spent in two months the sum of 400,000 francs (£16,000). Steinway produced a letter from Rossini affirming that his pianos were 'great as thunder and the storm and sweet as the piping of the nightingale on a spring night'; to which Chickering countered with Liszt's prayer that 'before dying he wished to see three things: the prairies of America, Niagara Falls and Chickering's pianos'.

33 Grand pianoforte by Steinway & Sons, London and New York, 1970. Compass AAA – c⁵. The left pedal operates the shift (*una corda*), the right the dampers; the centre pedal enables the player to sustain individual notes without raising the dampers throughout the instrument's compass.

They are normally single and double in the bass, double in the middle register, and triple in the treble. Their thickness varies from 0.70 to 1.20 and from 0.75 to 1.50 millimetres, depending on the maker. In theory a string ought to double in length with each octave it descends.[1] But if strings were in practice doubled, they would reach enormous lengths in the bass – at least seven yards – which would not only be unwieldly, but would require proportionately greater force from the hammers to set them vibrating. The dilemma is avoided in two ways, both of which have already been described: over-stringing and wrapping. These are only expedients but, nevertheless, they do give satisfactory results.

The strings are looped (at the far end of the instrument) to hitchpins embedded in the frame, and stretched back to the wrest-pins

[1] This increase is nothing compared to the increase required in the weight of bells, which must be doubled every time their note descends a major third.

109

which have square heads to facilitate tuning. Each of the wrest-pins can support a tension of over two hundred pounds. Between these two extremities, each string passes first between two metal studs, arranged obliquely so that the string deviates slightly in order to limit its vibration, and finally over a metal rail or bridge on the wrest-pin block. The vibrating part of the string is thus that section between the metal studs and the bridge. This arrangement is the same for the whole range of the strings, the vibrating part being short in the treble, while almost the entire length of the string is utilised in the bass. The point on the keyboard where the wrapped strings begin, and again where the cross-stringing starts, naturally divides the keyboard into distinct zones. Hence a fundamental of good piano construction consists in rendering these points of demarcation unnoticeable and achieving a homogenity of timbre from one end of the keyboard to the other.

The most delicate and complex part of the piano is the action, the muscles of this great body. Details of piano actions will be found in the separate illustrated section in the Appendix, starting on page 126.

The keyboard, enlarged by Erard in 1796 to five and a half octaves, reached six shortly afterwards in Germany. Today it is more than seven octaves. It rests on a special frame fixed on a ledge, comprising three wooden transverse beams, two fitted with studs to prevent the keys from getting out of alignment. They pivot over the central transverse.

As a general rule, there are only two pedals, the sustaining (or loud) pedal, which lifts all the dampers simultaneously, and the soft pedal, sometimes divided to produce both *piano* and *pianissimo*. The soft pedal effect is obtained in several ways. The pedal may bring the hammers near the strings thus diminishing the force of the blow; it may interpose between hammer and string a light strip of felt (as in the 'celeste' pedal) or, preferably and generally in the case of grand pianos, it may shift the hammers so that they strike only two strings instead of three (the *due corde, una corda* already discussed).[1]

In the chapter on the harpsichord, we spoke of tuning, noting that the old harpsichordists generally did the tuning themselves. It may be of interest to say a word about present-day practice. The string is stretched between the hitch-pin (which is fixed) and the wrest-pin, which has a square head that can be turned by means of a tuning-key. Each note being represented by several strings which must each be

[1] The true *una corda* and *due corde* effects are not, strictly speaking, possible on the modern piano which, as we have seen, has one string per note in the bass, two in the middle register and three in the treble. The device is much more effective on such an instrument as a Broadwood grand of *c* 1800, strung trichord throughout its compass. (Ed.)

tuned separately, the piano tuner isolates the one he wishes to work on by means of a wedge of felt or leather.

Tuning by twelve fifths scattered over seven octaves being inconvenient, the tuner crowds all these fifths into the range of an octave and a half, by means of a formula which varies with the individual tuner. The following is one of the most usual:

Starting with the initial A the tuner next finds its fifth, E. After that he tunes the fifth of E, namely B, drops an octave and then finds the fifth of B, that is F sharp. He continues thus alternately by fifths and octaves until he comes back to his original A. Afterwards he tunes the remaining notes on the keyboard by octaves.

Steinway instituted an even more compact formula for tuning:

The tuner is particularly careful to get a perfect tuning between octaves. As a concession to equal temperament, however, he must very slightly flatten his fifths and sharpen his fourths.

Today the piano has become an international instrument, not only because it has been internationally standardised, but also because the materials from which it is built come from all over the world. This is especially true of woods, of which about fifteen different varieties are used, according to their special properties.

Nevertheless, one cannot deny that there is such a thing as a 'national timbre' in different pianos; the French piano is not quite the same as a German piano, and the American piano is again different. This is not astonishing when we consider that different makers in the same country show radically opposed tendencies; and even between instruments coming from the same workshop and of the same model there are noticeable differences of tone, etc. Thus we find each virtuoso claiming a preference for this or that piano, according to his technique, his taste or style – not to mention other considerations less artistic and more substantial.

Unlike the first builders who were craftsmen working at home, beginning and finishing an instrument by themselves, the modern piano builder is a specialist, and his product is a factory product with its division of labour, mass production and the rest of it. Even the compression of the felt for the hammers, formerly a hand operation, is now done by giant compressing machines. The most noticeable feature in the evolution of piano manufacture during the twentieth century has been the strengthening of the instrument and the increase in its volume, in line with the tendencies of modern taste and to enable it to hold its own in the ever-growing modern orchestra. The various parts of the piano have been reinforced one after the other, and in consequence it has little by little acquired the heavy and powerful appearance which it shows today. The tension of the strings, now entirely of steel, which in 1850 corresponded to a weight of twelve tons, today exerts a pressure of over twenty, all supported by the metal frame.

The action has continued to grow in complexity, with its many composite parts made of different materials – wood, metal, felt, cloth – parts which though not oiled, must move easily, smoothly and without sound. Finally, this delicate and subtle mechanism must stand up to the test of a force which in the case of certain virtuosos approaches violence.[1] Although numerous systems of action are in use today, many of them only represent subtle variations of each other. The double escapement principle became standardised in the form of Herrburger and Schwander's action, which has today become public property. We have already mentioned that other makers besides Erard – such as Pleyel and Blüthner – had contributed their own adaptations of the same principle. Besides double escapement, single escapement is still used, the second escapement in this case being provided by springs.

With the growing power and general strengthening of the piano's mechanism, a greater amount of force has been demanded from the fingers of the player. In spite of counter-weights and every imaginable artifice, the increasing complexity of the action has made the required touch heavier. A weight of thirty grammes was sufficient to depress the keys on one of the Stein pianos which Mozart played. The modern piano requires at least twice that. Indeed, eighty grammes is considered

---

[1] Liszt especially was the terror of piano makers. When he played for the first time at the Gewandhaus Concerts in Leipzig his anger at not being able to obtain the French piano he had counted on caused him to break several of the hammers of the instrument which had replaced it.

the average pressure needed to depress the key of today. On the other hand, the human physique has not changed.[1] Many experiments have been made with the dimensions of the piano. The cumbersome concert grand was adapted to domestic use by the creation of models called 'semi-grands, quarter-grands and *crapauds*' (this nickname, which means 'toad', was given by Gounod to a small model by Pleyel, and the word has since passed into current French). These smaller 'grands' were achieved by shortening the strings – and thickening them proportionately – and by over-stringing. The pioneer in this work was Kaps of Dresden, who in 1865 reduced the grand piano to a length of five feet. His model had great success. More recently the reduction of the piano's size has been pushed to its limit. Both for reasons of economy and because of the smaller size of modern rooms, piano makers have exerted themselves to produce ingenious miniature uprights, which recall the 'piano-console' of Pape. The chief difficulty with these instruments has been to preserve their quality of tone. On the whole, the attempts have been successful, but it is clear that no further reduction in size can be made.

On the other hand, the awkward shape of the grand piano has frequently been attacked and efforts have been made to correct it. In 1794 Elias Schlengel built an oval piano. In 1804 G. Hoffmann of Berlin produced a symmetrically rounded piano. Blüthner exhibited a similar instrument in Paris in 1867. Carl Mand of Coblenz and Späthe of Gera followed, and the same shape continued to be used, especially by Günther of Brussels, for small grands, the concert models preserving their classic form.

In the external appearance of the piano, we see at work the same process of simplification that two centuries previously had standardised the violin. The violin, in its day, had also renounced sumptuous ornament, the side pieces inlaid with ivory and marquetry which had once been the pride of the Duiffoprugcars and the Tielkes. The same thing happened to the piano, only two hundred years later, and with a certain reluctance on the part of the decorators whose imagination seemed to linger longer on the greater decorative possibilities of the piano. The gilding and the brass, the draperies and the plumes, all the glitter and tinsel of the giraffe and pyramidal pianos disappeared with

[1] This reflection is not without importance when it is remembered, for example, that Beethoven's 'Appassionata' Sonata contains twelve thousand notes. It emphasises the really athletic nature of practice on an instrument to which relatively frail young women devote three or four hours of daily work. When Hummel stated that the piano 'less than any other instrument is capable of injuring the health of the weakest' we must keep in mind the difference between the old Viennese action to which he referred and our own.

them; but the upright and the grand were not altogether spared. Grand 'pianos de luxe' were made, ornamented with mother-of-pearl, jasper, malachite, alabaster and marble. Erard exhibited a piano gilded all over. Pape built for the Duchess of Berry a piano covered with ivory slabs as big as handkerchiefs, obtained by means of a circular saw which 'peeled' the ivory tusk as one peels an apple. Presentation pianos, offered to important personages, and instruments designed for exhibitions were similarly built at enormous expense. The most flagrant errors were made in such anachronisms, as designing a piano case in styles older than the piano itself. (A Louis XIV piano is, after all, as absurd as a 'Renaissance' locomotive.) American makers reached the limits of extravagance with 'Gothic' pianos. More recent than the grand, the upright piano more or less escaped this decorative orgy, but not entirely. Not many years ago there were still uprights with branched candlesticks in gilded brass and busts of musicians on brackets. But today all this has disappeared. Piano cases, stripped to their essentials, have taken on the sober and ascetic appearance admired by the modern interior decorator.

For the sake of completeness we must glance at the many exceptional pianos which we owe to the ingenuity or the fantasy of inventors. Welcker von Gontershausen listed a number of such novelties in his book *Der Klavierbau* (1870), and still more were described by de Pontécoulant in his accounts of his visits to the first world exhibitions. The majority of such innovations have, however, come to nothing or at most are gathering dust in our museums. It is extremely difficult to overcome tradition or inveterate technical habits, even in favour of valuable improvements.[1]

Innovations which had no immediate usefulness, instruments which required a musical literature not yet written naturally had very little chance of survival; and many such inventions were either unknown to composers or not utilised by them.[2]

---

[1] Thus the horn has no reason for its circular shape except tradition. It is derived from the mediæval hunting horn which was curved to imitate the curved horn of primitive animals. With the progressive lengthening of the tube the curve of the horn necessarily ended in a circle; but it could just as well have become the shape of the letter S. On the other hand, the modern trumpet, instead of being straight, could have been made circular.

[2] A particularly characteristic example may be mentioned. The viol family of instruments was formerly complete. Its modern successor, the violin family, is not, however, complete because of the disappearance of the tenor violin which leaves a space between the viola and the violoncello. Thus there was nothing more logical, in principle, than Hermann Ritter's reconstruction of a rational quartet, consisting of a single violin, a viola, a tenor violin and a cello. But the combination had no chance of success because thousands of works had already been written for the classic quartet with its two violins, viola and cello, and modern composers follow the example of their predecessors.

A certain number of inventions were inspired by the discoveries made in the realms of harmonic analysis by Helmholtz, which were published by him in his celebrated *Lehre von den Tonempfindungen* in 1863, and subsequently translated into every modern language. Helmholtz's work on acoustics completed the discovery of harmonic resonance made by the French scientist Savart in 1700, that is to say, at a time when acoustic resonators, which today enable us to detect harmonics, were still unknown.[1] Among the ideas inspired by Helmholtz's discoveries was Steinway's of using that part of the string not set in vibration by the hammer – in other words the section beyond the bridge – to enrich the vibrating string with its harmonics. Collard had already tried to apply this principle in London in 1822. Stein had also made a sensation by building a piano fitted with a stop which controlled a set of supplementary strings vibrating sympathetically. In his *Aliquot-Flügel*, Blüthner doubled each string with a second, tuned at the octave; Kaps of Dresden divided each string into equal parts by a bridge, one part being struck, the other being left free to vibrate harmonically.

The piano was combined with a number of other instruments, chiefly with its predecessor and rival, the harpsichord. According to the *Encyclopédie* ('Music', article *Clavecin*, by Framery), Silbermann in Freiberg and Péronard in Paris, are said to have built such instruments – on Schobert's suggestion – by combining a harpsichord with a piano action played by a pedal board. Erard, Stodart and Stein built similar instruments without the pedal board.

The piano, with its unstable tuning, was even combined with reed and pipe instruments, the pitch of which is (comparatively) invariable. Just as there had been 'organised harpsichords', there were piano-organs. The inventory of Madame du Barry's furniture mentions one of these instruments. Liszt, in Weimar, conceived the notion of a similar instrument, but considerably developed. At his request Berlioz gave the organ builder Alexandre, of Paris, an order to build the instrument, furnished with three keyboards, sixteen stops and a pedal board. Delivered in 1854, it is now in the Altenburg museum in Weimar.

Piano-organs were also built in London by Longman and Broderip. Today the piano-organ has given way to the piano-harmonium, in which the pipes are replaced by freely vibrating reeds (the prototype being Schmidt's 'piano-harmonica'). Debain's 'piano-concert' (Paris, 1877) combined the piano with the organ, the harmonium and the

---

[1] Dumont, in his eulogy on the harpsichord made by Jean Couchet for de Chambonnières, notes and praises the enrichment of timbre lent to the vibrating string by the sympathetic vibration of a second string tuned at the octave.

harmonicorde (an instrument invented by Kaufmann of Dresden in 1809, in which the strings were vibrated by a rotating cylinder). In Belgium, Cloetens's *orphéal* was a piano which ingeniously produced astonishing approximations of the horn, the cello, etc., while the same maker's *luthéal* combined the piano with the harpsichord. Lenz and Houdard, in Paris, constructed a *piano scandé*, in which any one section of the keyboard could be made to stand out above the others. Philippe de Girard, also of Paris, made pianos with octave couplers (1805) as well as a *trémolophone*, an idea taken up again in 1835 by Pape, and achieved more recently by other means, by Cloetens. Mention should also be made of the *clavi-harpe* invented by the Dietz family of Paris and Brussels.

The arrangement of the piano keyboard has been criticised as being perpendicular to the arms and hands of the executant only in the middle register, while in the treble and bass he must strike the notes at an angle, endangering his precision. In 1780 Neuhaus invented a circular keyboard to remedy this defect; the idea was revived in 1824 by Staufer and Haudinger, and in 1910 by Clutsam. The same reason inspired Wölfel's arched piano (Paris c 1840) and Bühl's *Bogen-Klavier*, and finally the *Strahlen-Klavier*, which had a rectangular keyboard, but with keys radiating towards the centre.

However, the chief and fundamental fault of the keyboard still remains its illogical and irregular arrangement of keys, a heritage of its slow and groping historical development. We have already explained, in discussing the clavichord and equal temperament, how the original diatonic keyboard was made chromatic by the addition first of the flattened seventh note (B flat), then of the sharpened fourth (F sharp), and finally of the other 'black' notes. If our system of twelve semitones had been instituted all at once, the keyboard would have been adapted to it, and each key given the same importance. But this was not the case. Not only did the development take place by stages, but the chromatic notes for a long while had only a limited use, because of the rare employment of distant keys. From the moment when, thanks to equal temperament, the composer's invention could roam at will among all keys and modulate freely, the disadvantage of the traditional keyboard became apparent, not only in the difficulty of playing between the black keys (especially for fat fingers), but in the diversity of fingering for the same phrases and the same scale-passages in different keys.

Efforts to bring order to this chaos were defeated by the weight of tradition. At the end of the eighteenth century Johann Rohleder of Friedland had constructed a keyboard in which the diatonic and the chromatic notes alternated regularly. In 1811 the German Krause made all the keys the same level and the same colour. In 1829 the Frenchman Gaussin created his 'isotone' with a chromatic keyboard composed of all white keys, while Schiedmayer of Stuttgart alternated black and white keys in keyboards on which all scales could be played with one of two fingerings, depending on whether the scale began with a white or a black key.

The most radical innovation – and one which caused most stir – was that of the Hungarian Paul von Janko, built by Ibach of Barmen. In 1882 Janko replaced the entire traditional keyboard by a quadrangular keyboard composed of six rows of narrow, short and rounded keys, rows number one, three and five alternating with rows number two, four and six. The fingering of every scale is the same. The intervals, being closer together than on the ordinary keyboard and the octave comprising only seven notes instead of twelve, a simple movement of the wrist replaces distant jumps. In 1910 Paul Perzina devised a reversible version of the Janko keyboard, which could be used in conjunction with a conventional keyboard, on the same instrument. The Janko keyboard excited great interest in Germany and Austria. Keyboard studies were composed for it and a special class to teach it was started at the Scharwenka Conservatoire in Berlin. Today it is forgotten; the great music publishers, whose publications furnished with traditional fingering it menaced, were not, perhaps, without influence. / Again with the improvement of the keyboard in mind, attempts have been made to prevent the fingers slipping on keys of glossy ivory and its substitutes, celluloid, bakelite and imitation ivory, chiefly by the use of hardened rubber.

Also, for various reasons, pianos with double keyboards have been built. Stein produced such a piano which was called *vis-à-vis*, and about 1895 the firm of Pleyel made a rectangular piano with two keyboards arranged in the same way, with a double set of strings and a double action, but a single soundboard. As a rule, double keyboards corresponded to different tunings. The *Dittanaclasis* of M. Müller (Vienna, 1801) joined together two upright pianos, the keyboard of one tuned an octave higher than the other. The inconvenience of playing between the black keys gave the Belgian inventor, Pierre Hans (1917), the idea of a piano with two keyboards, the second of which was tuned to a semitone above the first.

In 1927 the Hungarian Emanuel Móor, in his 'Duplex Coupler Grand Pianoforte', revived Müller's idea, but with the two keyboards coupled at will and the back part of the white keys raised to the level

117

of the black keys to facilitate *glissando*. Finally, in the piano with reversible keyboards (a real monster, actually superimposing two grand pianos), constructed in 1876 by Mangeot in Paris, on the specifications of the Polish pianist Joseph Wieniawski (1837-1912), the second keyboard runs from right to left, so that its bass falls immediately over the treble of the first keyboard and both can be played by the same hand.[1]

The subdivision of the octave into intervals smaller than a semitone has given rise to corresponding subdivisions of the keyboard. The most recent example is the quarter-tone piano invented by Aloïs Haba of Prague. It comprises two keyboards, one normal, the other tuned a quarter-tone higher. A class to teach this piano was created in the Prague Conservatoire, where Aloïs Haba, in 1923, began a course of compositions in quarter-tones and sixth-tones.

The action of the pedals has not given rise to many variations. But, in the *anémocorde*, whose eventful history Welcker von Gonterhausen has related, pedals were used for regulating currents of air which excited the vibration of strings.[2] Inspired by the *anémocorde*, Henri Herz devised a pedal to produce *crescendi* and *decrescendi* by the action of a current of air.

In 1824 Streicher built an upright piano with an octave pedal which doubled the note struck with its octave. To the two usual grand piano pedals, Steinway added a third, which permitted a single note to be sustained to the exclusion of the rest. (This effect is precisely what in harmony is called a 'pedal'.) The idea had already been used by the inventor of the harmonium, Alexandre Debain, and even in the piano itself by Boisselot of Marseilles in 1844, Pleyel and Montal. In Belgium, Smulders invented his 'expressive' pedal which drew the hammers further back from the strings, requiring more pressure to depress the keys.

---

[1] This piano with reversible keyboards was shown at the World Exhibition in Paris in 1878 by the Russian pianist Zarembski. Mangeot built six specimens of the instrument (of which one is in the museum of the Brussels Conservatoire) and also a few uprights on the same system.

[2] Johann Jacob Schnell, a native of Württemberg who worked in Paris with the title of 'Maker to the Countess of Artois', had laboured for years at the construction of the *anémocorde*, an instrument in which a bellows, worked by pedals and regulated by stops to control intensity, sent a current of air through copper tubes against silk-wrapped strings (three to a note). Marie-Antoinette is said to have offered Schnell 100,000 louis plus a bonus of 50,000 livres for this instrument; but not possessing that sum at the moment she asked him to keep the instrument for her. When the Revolution broke out, Schnell nearly lost his head but his wife saved him thanks to the *anémocorde*. The couple returned to Germany and finally the *anémocorde* was sold in England.

The piano copied the organ in the addition of a pedal-board, notably in the 'pianoforte-organistico' of the Abbé J. Trentino (1817), followed by a similar instrument by Pierre Erard (which was reproduced by his nephew in 1839 and in 1844). In 1843, the London maker Louis Schoen built Schumann an upright and Mendelssohn a grand, both pianos with pedal-boards having twenty-nine keys. Schumann composed his 'Sketches for Pedal-Piano', Op. 58 in 1845, and attached much importance to them. Many pedal-pianos are said to have been in use in Paris in 1845. Pleyel built pianos with movable pedal-boards which the French pianist Delaborde tried in vain to popularise in Germany.

Pleyel and other builders devised mechanisms in which a single key simultaneously played several notes. Pleyel also invented a special instrument, the *molliphone,* in which the volume of tone could be reduced to the minimum.

Transposing pianos were built on many systems. The classic system, namely, that by which the keyboard shifts, is said to have been introduced by Silbermann. In 1788 an organ builder from Amsterdam by the name of Torenberg received a medal and a prize for a piano which could be lowered one or two octaves in the bass. An instrument by Roller and Blanchet (1824) could in this way change its tonality from one up to five semitones. A transposing piano was made in Brussels in 1836 by Rouchette. Pleyel created a transposing attachment in several keys, which was applicable to all pianos.

Numerous systems for registering (or 'stenographical') pianos have been devised, notably by the German Unger (1716-80), who created the first of such instruments, and who was followed by Creed, Carrère, Guérin, Eisenmerger, Pape, Adorno and Tesselhof. Finally, silent keyboards were made for the technical purpose of practice (a principle condemned by Schumann, who complained that 'a mute cannot teach us how to speak'). The best of these silent keyboards seems to have been introduced in 1892 by the American, Virgil.

We will not attempt to list exhaustively the many automatic instruments: the 'pianola', the 'phonola', the 'odéola', the 'welte-mignon', the 'duo-art' and the other player pianos which enable a work to be played according to the executant's own taste, or else reproduce an interpretation recorded by a famous pianist. All are based on the principle of a roll of paper pierced with holes which enable a passage of air, acting on a valve, to set the keys in motion. Launched towards the end of the nineteenth century, the player-piano quickly achieved a considerable vogue, and, under different names, ingeniously plagiarised from each other, became widely popular, especially in Anglo-Saxon countries. Already threatened by the invention of the gramophone, the player-piano was to receive its death blow from the radio.

*As a piece of furniture, the piano assumed many shapes and forms. The Englishman Robert Stodart, a disciple of John Broadwood, patented a piano in the form of a bookcase. In Paris, Pape created square pianos in diverse shapes, hexagonal, table-pianos, piano-consoles, circular, oval and polygonal pianos. Erard invented a 'column-piano'. We have mentioned the symmetrical grand piano. Pianos were also made in the shape of an antique lyre, with the case hollowed out above, enabling the executant to see over it and to follow the conductor; others with keyboards which could be raised or lowered – which, modernised and improved, have come back into fashion, and in certain cases, render great service. Portable pianos were invented. like that of the Abbé Trentino and the 'orphica' of Röllig (Vienna, 1795), especially designed for use out of doors, and the portable pianos of the old Brussels builders, the Daniel brothers and Adrien.

Just as there had been travelling harpsichords so there were travelling pianos. J-M. Schmahl of Ulm built instruments of this sort about 1770, little pianos in the shape of a couched harp with a single row of strings, transposable by means of a shifting keyboard. An example of one of these instruments is preserved in a Berlin Museum, and is said to have been Mozart's travelling piano. Pianos were adapted for distant expeditions. As early as 1771 Lemme of Brunswick had had the idea of reinforcing soundboards destined for Batavia with a veneer of compressed wood. After him, Jenkins constructed a 'cottage piano' which could be made larger or smaller at will. Blanchet built small instruments for the small steam-ships of his day. Pianos divisible into two parts were made which could be carried by mule-pack across the Andes. In Paris, Kriegelstein compressed a bijou grand piano of $7\frac{1}{4}$ octaves into the dimensions of $4'\ 11'' \times 4'\ 4''$. It is strange that, generally speaking, small pianos with miniature keyboards for children have not been built, like the half and three-quarter sized violins made for this purpose. Only comparatively recently the idea was taken up by Balthasar-Florence, of Namur, and also by Steinway.

Finally, the piano was combined with other pieces of furniture, especially with bureaux, like the 'piano-bureau' belonging to François Fétis, first director of the Brussels Conservatoire, an Erard dated 1819. Or it was furnished with a music stand for conducting (convenient in the theatre when the recitative was accompanied by the *maestro al cembalo*), and a box containing make-up, powder, rouge, a bottle of perfume – for the use of opera singers.

120

Because of its complexity, the piano is, apart from the organ, the musical instrument which is most susceptible to improvement and modification of all kinds. When we hear the square pianos of the last century (themselves a hundred years later than Cristofori's invention), it is hard to believe that they could have satisfied the great virtuosos and musicians of their day. Nor can we imagine where the efforts and ingenuity of piano builders will have led us a hundred years hence. Compared with their ancestors, the beautiful instruments of today naturally seem to us the ideal of perfection. But each generation tends to consider its own accomplishments in every department the final state of perfection. This is rarely true, and it may not be true of the piano. In view of the precipitous evolution of music in the last few decades, and if it is true that instruments adapt themselves to contemporary taste and style, no one can foresee the keyboard instruments which the music of the future will demand.

Appendix

Figure 1 Clavichord action

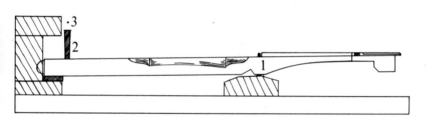

1 Key
2 Tangent
3 String (seen end on)

When the key (1) is depressed, the brass tangent (2) is raised and presses against the string (3), making the length of string between the tangent and the bridge sound, the shorter length between the tangent and the nut being damped by a strip of felt woven between the strings. When the key is released the felt automatically damps the whole length of the string between the nut and bridge.

Figure 2 Harpsichord jack

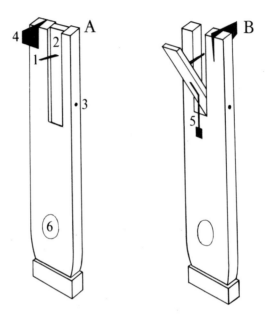

A shows the jack in its striking position
B shows the jack on its return, after plucking the string

1 Plectrum (quill, leather etc.)
2 Tongue
3 Pivot
4 Damper
5 Spring
6 Weight

When the key is depressed its far end pushes the jack upwards and the plectrum (1) plucks the string. When the key is released the plectrum is enabled to slide past the string by means of the hinged tongue (2), the spring (traditionally of hog's bristle) (5) returning the tongue to its upright position immediately after the plectrum has passed the string, and the damper (of cloth or felt) (4) silencing the note at the same time.

124

Figure 3 Action of a two-manual harpsichord (Kirckman, 1755)

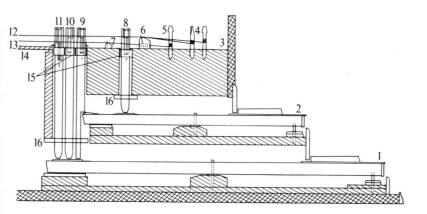

1 Lower manual
2 Upper manual
3 Wrest-plank
4 Eight-foot wrest-pins
5 Four-foot wrest-pins
6 Eight-foot nut
7 Four-foot nut
8 Lute stop jack
9 Eight-foot jack, both manuals
10 Eight-foot jack, lower manual
11 Eight-foot jack, lower manual
12 Eight-foot strings
13 Four-foot strings
14 Soundboard
15 Jack slides (movable)
16 Jack guides (fixed)

Figure 4 Cristofori's grand pianoforte action of 1711

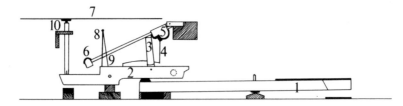

1 Key
2 Intermediate lever
3 Escapement
4 Escapement spring
5 Hammer butt
6 Hammer head
7 String
8 Silk strings
9 Shanks to which the silk strings are attached
10 Damper

When the key (1) is depressed it raises the intermediate lever (2) which, in its turn, raises the escapement (3) which acts upon the hammer (5, 6). At the moment when the hammer is jerked up and strikes the string (7) the escapement 'escapes'. After this, the hammer does not fall back directly upon the escapement, but upon the spring (4), which keeps it nearer the string. When the finger releases the key, the hammer drops into the sheath formed by the two silk strings (8) which are supported by shanks (9). The damper (10) normally presses against the string, but frees the string to vibrate when the key – and hence the intermediate lever to which the damper is attached – is depressed. When the key is released the damper again presses against the string.

Figure 5 Cristofori's grand pianoforte action of 1720

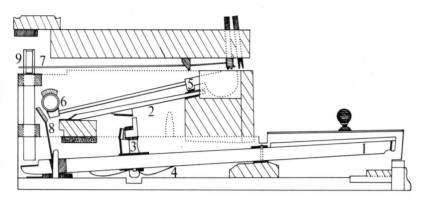

1 Key
2 Intermediate lever
3 Escapement
4 Escapement spring
5 Hammer butt
6 Hammer head
7 String
8 Check
9 Damper

This is a more sophisticated version of Cristofori's 1711 action. The escapement or jack (3) raises the intermediate lever (2), which propels the hammer (5, 6) against the string (7) and then 'escapes' and returns to its previous position. The hammer head (6) is then caught by the check (8) and prevented from rebounding against the string. The damper (9) rests on top of the string but is raised by the far end of the key when the latter is depressed.

Figure 6 Simple form of German action (J. G. Mahr)

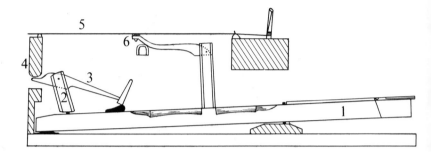

1 Key
2 Sheath (*kapsel*)
3 Hammer
4 Ledge (*prelleiste*)
5 String
6 Damper

When the key (1) is depressed the hammer butt engages with the *prelleiste* (4) and the hammer head is jerked upwards to the string (5). The movement of the key also allows the damper (6) to withdraw slightly from its position beneath the string.

128

Figure 7 Improved German grand pianoforte action (Stein, 1786)

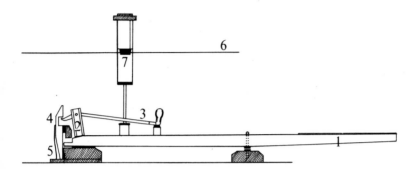

1 Key
2 Sheath (*kapsel*)
3 Hammer
4 Escapement
5 Spring
6 String
7 Damper

In this more developed form of the German action the *prelleiste*
incorporates an escapement mechanism, which is independent of the
rest of the action. When the key (1) is depressed, the end of the
hammer shaft catches in a slot cut out of the escapement (4). The
hammer (3), thus raised, strikes the string (6) and then falls back again.
But the end of the hammer-shaft rests against the escapement, above
and outside the slot. When the key is released, the escapement draws
back, permitting the hammer again to take its place in the slot of the
escapement. This is pushed forward by the spring (5). The damper (7)
merits particular attention. It is independent of the rest of the action
being worked by a separate jack fixed to each key. The felt is in the
shape of a wedge. As the strings are double for each note, the point of the
wedge penetrates between the two strings, damping them equally. When
the damper is raised, it withdraws from both strings at once and falls back
between them by its own weight.

Figure 8 Simple English square pianoforte action (Pohlmann, 1784)

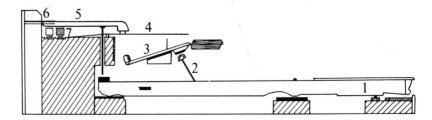

1 Key
2 Jack
3 Hammer
4 String
5 Damper
6 Whalebone spring
7 'Forte' stop

There is no escapement. The hammer (3) is propelled towards the string (4) by the jack (2), whose height is adjustable. The damper (5) is hinged to the back of the case and pressed against the string by a whalebone spring (6). The damper is raised by a thin stick activated by the far end of the key when the latter is depressed, or can be raised indefinitely by means of a wedge-shaped lever (7) operated by a hand-stop, which has the same effect as a sustaining or 'loud' pedal.

130

Figure 9 Simple English square pianoforte action with under-dampers (Broadwood, 1783)

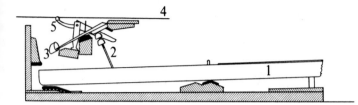

1 Key
2 Jack
3 Hammer
4 String
5 Damper

The principle is similar to the action of Figure 8, but the dampers (of brass) act on the strings from below and are incorporated in the hammer mechanism. The jack (2) has a leather-covered wooden head in two parts, the lower activating the damper (5) and the higher the hammer (3).

Figure 10 English grand pianoforte action (Broadwood, 1795)

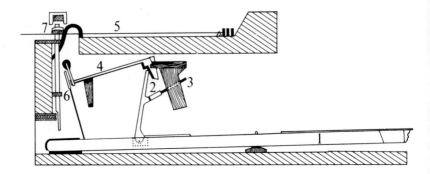

1 Key
2 Escapement
3 Regulating screw
4 Hammer
5 String
6 Check
7 Damper

The escapement is regulated by the screw (3). The derivation of this action from Cristofori's of 1720 (Figure 5) can easily be seen by comparing the two diagrams.

Figure 11 English square pianoforte action (Broadwood, 1815)

1 Key
2 Escapement ('Hopper')
3 Regulating screw
4 Under-hammer
5 Hammer
6 String
7 Damper crank
8 Damper

Escapement is effected by a 'hopper' (short for 'grasshopper') first patented by John Geib, which has a built-in regulating screw (3). The damper (8) is attached by a leather hinge to the damper crank (7), which is itself similarly hinged to the back of the case, and is raised by the far end of the key (1) when the latter is depressed.

Figure 12 Taskin's action of 1787

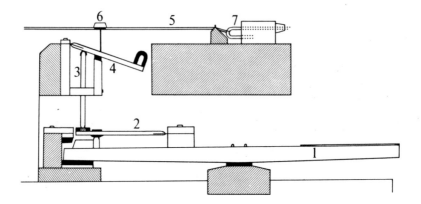

1 Key
2 Intermediate lever
3 Jack
4 Hammer
5 String
6 Damper
7 Hook for tuning

When the key (1) is depressed, it raises the intermediate lever (2), which acts upon the jack (3), which impels the hammer (4) against the string (5). At the same time the damper (6), which is fixed obliquely to the shank of the hammer and normally rests against the string, is raised. When the key is released, the hammer falls again by its own weight and the damper again rests against the string.

Figure 13 Erard's single escapement action of 1795 (improved 1816)

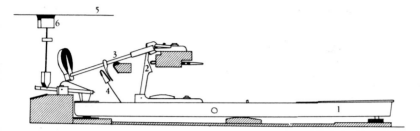

1 Key
2 Intermediate lever forming the escapement
3 Hammer
4 Check
5 String
6 Damper

When the key (1) is depressed, it raises the lever (2), which, acting on the butt, causes the hammer (3) to strike the string (5). Immediately afterwards the head of the lever escapes from the butt, slipping in a groove. The distance between the hammer head and the string depends directly upon how far the key is pressed down. When the key is released progressively, the hammer drops away from the string, but also progressively. When the key is completely released, the hammer falls back into the position shown after having brushed against the hammer check (4), which acts as a sort of brake. The damper (6), which, at rest, is kept against the string by means of a spring, drops when the key is depressed.

Figure 14 Erard's double escapement action of 1822

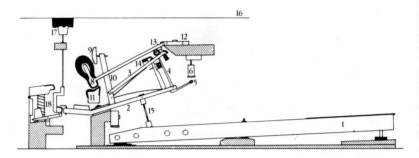

1 Key	11 Hammer rest
2 Intermediate lever	12 Hammer rail
3 Repetition lever	13 'T' of the double-escapement
4 Hopper or escapement	14 Screw to regulate the double-
5 Hopper spur	escapement
6 Escapement button	15 Screw to regulate the arc des-
7 Hammer butt	cribed by the hammer
8 Hammer head	16 String
9 Check	17 Damper
10 Shank of hammer check	18 Pedal spring

When the key (1) is depressed, it raises the intermediate lever (2) by means of a wormed shaft (15), which regulates the course of the hammer. The intermediate lever acts simultaneously upon the repetition lever (3) and the hopper or escapement (4). The repetition lever acts upon the butt (7) and jerks the hammer (8) against the string (16), while the hopper 'escapes' from the butt, its spur (5) having struck against the escapement button (6). When the key is not completely released, the hammer is held by the check (9), in this way falling back from the string only a fraction of an inch which permits quick repetition of a note. If, on the contrary, the key is completely released, the hammer falls back to its original position on the hammer rest (11). The damper (17), in repose, is held against the string by a counterweight. It releases the string when the key is depressed and rocks the intermediate lever. Independently of this separate damper action, all the dampers can be raised at once by the sustaining pedal, the spring of which is shown at (18).

Figure 15 Erard's upright action

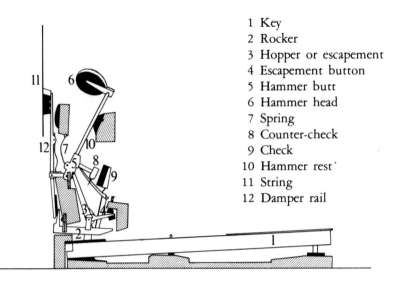

1 Key
2 Rocker
3 Hopper or escapement
4 Escapement button
5 Hammer butt
6 Hammer head
7 Spring
8 Counter-check
9 Check
10 Hammer rest'
11 String
12 Damper rail

When the key (1) is depressed it raises the rocker (2), on which the hopper or escapement (3) rests. The hopper, working in a groove in the hammer butt (5), throws the hammer head (6) against the string (11). When the hammer is about to strike the string, the tip of the horizontal part of the hopper touches the escapement button (4), which forces the top of the vertical section of the hopper to slip from the groove of the hammer butt. When the hammer has struck the string, it falls back by its own weight assisted by the spring (7). The counter-check (8) falls back against the check (9) and thus gently allows the hammer to come back against the hammer rest (10). When the key is depressed, the rocker also acts upon the damper rail (12), freeing the string to vibrate. As in the preceding example explaining Erard's double escapement action, all the dampers can be released simultaneously by the sustaining pedal. The action illustrated is known as 'under-damper' action, as the damper acts beneath the hammer. In the 'over-damper' action the damper, attached to the extremity of a brass rod shaped like a bayonet, acts above the point where the hammer strikes. It is generally considered less efficient than the present arrangement.

137

Figure 16 Modern grand pianoforte action (Herrburger Brooks)

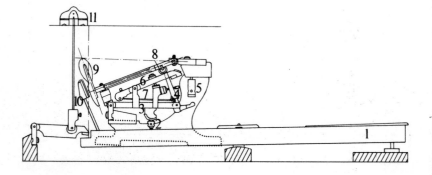

1 Key	7 Repetition spring
2 Capstan screw	8 Roller
3 Support or wippen	9 Hammer
4 Jack	10 Check
5 Set-off button	11 Damper
6 Repetition lever	

When the key (1) is depressed, the adjustable capstan screw (2) raises the wippen (3) on which the jack (4) is pivoted. The tip of the jack, passing through a slot in the repetition lever (6) – which is positioned by the adjustable repetition spring (7) and an adjustable screw at the pivot end of the hammer shank (9) – engages with the leather-covered roller (8) fixed to the base of the hammer shank, escaping to the rear (keyboard end) of it at a point determined by the regulation of the set-off button (5) and other regulation adjustments, enabling the hammer to fall back after striking the string and allowing the wippen, together with its associated parts, to re-position itself for the next depression of the key.

138

Figure 17 Modern upright pianoforte action (Herrburger Brooks)

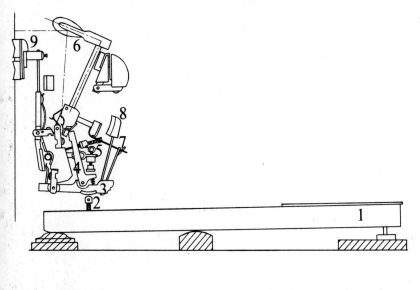

1 Key	6 Hammer
2 Capstan screw	7 Tape
3 Support or wippen	8 Check
4 Jack	9 Damper
5 Set-off button	

When the key (1) is depressed, the adjustable capstan screw (2) raises the wippen (3) on which the jack (4) is pivoted. The jack raises the butt of the hammer (6), 'escaping' just before the latter has actually struck the string, at a point determined by the setting of the adjustable set-off button (5). The return of the hammer is assisted by the tape, (7), which brings it to rest against the check (8), positioning it in readiness for the next blow. The far end of the wippen activates the damper (9), withdrawing it from the string just before the hammer strikes it and allowing it to return as soon as the key is released.

Bibliography

ADLUNG, Jacob: *Musica mechanica organoedi.* Berlin, 1768/Kassel, 1931.

AGRICOLA, Martin: *Musica instrumentalis deudsch.* Wittenberg, 1529.

ANDERSON, Emily: *The Letters of Mozart and his family.* London, 1938.

ANDRÉ, Karl August: *Der Klavierbau.* Frankfurt, 1855.

AUERBACH, Cornelia: *Die deutsche Clavichordkunst des 18. Jahrhunderts.* Kassel, 1930.

BACH, Carl Philipp Emanuel: *Versuch über die wahre Art das Clavier zu spielen.* Berlin, 1753. Trs. William J. Mitchell as *Essay on the true art of playing keyboard instruments.* New York, 1949.

BAINES, Anthony (ed.): *Musical instruments through the ages.* London, 1961.

BECKER, Carl Ferdinand: *Hausmusik in Deutschland im 16., 17. und 18. Jahrhundert.* Leipzig, 1840.

141

BEIJNUM, B. van: *Bouw en geschiedenis van het Klavier.* Rotterdam, 1932.

BESSARABOFF, Nicholas: *Ancient European musical instruments.* Boston, 1941.

BIE, Oscar: *Das Klavier und seine Meister.* Munich, 1898. Trs E. E. Kellett and E. W. Naylor as *The pianoforte and pianoforte players.* London, 1899.

BLONDEL, S.: *Histoire anecdotique du piano.* Paris, 1880.

BLONDEL, S.: Article on the piano in *Encyclopédie de la musique et Dictionnaire du Conservatoire.* Paris, n.d.

BLÜTHNER, Julius and GRETCHEL, H.: *Der Pianofortebau.* Leipzig, 1872/1909.

BOALCH, Donald: *Makers of the harpsichord and clavichord, 1440-1840.* London, 1956.

BODKY, E.: *Der Vortrag alter Klaviermusik.* Berlin, 1932.

BORREN, Charles van den: *Les origines de la musique de clavecin en Angleterre.* Brussels, 1912.

BORREN, Charles van den: *Les musiciens belges en Angleterre à l'époque de la Renaissance.* Brussels, 1913.

BORREN, Charles van den: *Les origines de la musique de clavecin aux Pays-Bas.* Brussels, 1914.

BREIDERT, Friedrich and FREYSE, Conrad: *Verzeichnis der Sammlung alter Musikinstrumente im Bachhause zu Eisenach.* Leipzig, 1939.

BRINSMEAD, Edgar: *History of the pianoforte.* London, 1889.

BRIQUEVILLE, Eugène de: *Le clavecin de Mme. du Barry et le piano de la Reine Marie-Antoinette.* Paris, 1892.

BRIQUEVILLE, Eugène de: *Les anciens instruments de musique.* Paris, 1884.

BRIQUEVILLE, Eugène de: *Les ventes d'instruments.* Paris, 1908.

BROWN, Crosby: *Catalogue of keyboard musical instruments in the Crosby Brown Collection.* New York, 1903.

BRUNNER, Hans: *Das Klavierklangideal Mozarts und die Klaviere seiner Zeit.* Augsburg, 1933.

BÜCH, Francis: *Du piano.* Rouen, 1869.

BUCHNER, Alexander (Trs. Iris Unwin): *Musical instruments through the ages.* London, 1961.

BURBURE, Léon de: *Recherches sur les facteurs de clavecins et les luthiers d'Anvers depuis le XVIe jusqu'au XIXe siècle.* Brussels, 1863.

BURNEY, Charles (ed. Percy Scholes): *An eighteenth-century musical tour in Central Europe and the Netherlands.* London, 1959.

CASELLA, Alfredo: *Il pianoforte.* Rome and Milan, 1937.
CHOUQUET, Gustave: *La Musée du Conservatoire National de Musique.* Paris, 1875/1844-1903.
CLEMENCIC, René (Trs. David Hermges): *Old musical instruments.* London, 1968.
CLOSSON, Ernest: *La facture des instruments de musique en Belgique.* Brussels, 1935.
COLT, C. F.: *The Colt Clavier Collection at Bethersden, Kent.* Portsmouth, n.d.
COUPERIN, François: *L'Art de toucher le clavecin.* Paris, 1716-17.

DALE, William: *Tschudi the Harpsichord Maker.* London, 1913.
DOLGE, Alfred: *Pianos and their makers.* Covina (California), 1911.
DOLMETSCH, Arnold: *The interpretation of the music of the XVII and XVIII centuries.* London, 1915/44.
DUPONT, W.: *Geschichte der musikalischen Temperatur.* Kassel, 1935.

ELLIS, Alexander: *The history of musical pitch.* London, 1880.
ENCYCLOPÉDIE MÉTHODIQUE: *Arts et Métiers, Vol. IV, Instruments de musique et lutherie.* Paris, 1751-2, 1776-7.
ENCYCLOPÉDIE MÉTHODIQUE: *Dictionnaire de Musique.* art. 'Clavecin' (Hüllmandel) and 'Piano' (de Momigny). Paris, 1782-1832.
ENGEL, Carl: *Catalogue of the special exhibition of ancient musical instruments.* London, 1872.
ENGEL, Carl: *A descriptive catalogue of the musical instruments in the South Kensington Museum.* London, 1874.
ERARD, Pierre: *Perfectionnements apportés dans le mécanisme du piano par les Erard.* Paris, 1834.
ERARD, Frères: *Les grandes usines de Turgan.* Paris, 1887.
ERARD, Frères: *La maison Erard, 1780-1903, ses origines, ses inventions, ses travaux.* Paris, 1903.

FARRENC, Louise: 'Esquisse de l'histoire du piano' in *Trésor des pianistes.* Paris, 1861.
FILLMORE, J-C.: *History of pianoforte music.* 1883.
FISCHHOF, J.: *Versuch einer Geschichte des Klavierbaues.* Vienna, 1853.

GALLINI, Natale and Franco: *Museo degli Strumenti Musicali, Castello Sforzesco, Milano.* Milan, 1963.
GALPIN SOCIETY; *British musical instruments (Arts Council Exhibition, August 1951).* London, 1951.

GALPIN, Francis: *Old English instruments of music.* London, 1910/1921/1932.

GALPIN, Francis: *A textbook of European musical instruments.* London, 1937.

GARNAULT, P.: *Histoire et influence du tempérament.* Nice, 1829.

GEORGII, Walter: *Klaviermusik, Geschichte von dem Anfang bis zu Gegenwart.* Berlin, 1941.

GOEBEL, J.: *Grundzüge des modernen Klavierbaues.* 1925.

GÖHLINGER, Franz August: *Geschichte des Klavichords.* Basel, 1910.

GOUGH, Hugh: 'Clavichord', art. in *Grove's Dictionary.* London, 1954.

GOUGH, Hugh: *The classical grand pianoforte.* Proceedings of the R.M.A., Vol. LXXVII, 1951.

GUCHTENAERE, M. de: *Le piano.* Ghent, 1924.

HAAS, Robert: *Bach und Mozart in Wien.* Vienna, 1951.

HAMMERICH, Angul: *Das Musikhistorische Museum zu Kopenhagen.* Copenhagen, 1911.

HARDING, Rosamond: *The Piano-Forte, its history traced to the Great Exhibition of 1851.* Cambridge, 1933.

HARDING, Rosamond: 'Harpsichord', art. in *Grove's Dictionary.* London, 1954.

HARDING, Rosamond: 'Pianoforte', art. in *Grove's Dictionary.* London, 1954.

HARRISON, Frank and RIMMER, Joan: *European musical instruments.* London, 1964.

HAUTERIVE, G-M.: *La facture du piano.* Brussels, 1939.

HEMEL, V. van: *Het Klavier.* Antwerp, 1941.

HERTZ, Eva: *J. A. Stein: ein Beitrag zur Geschichte des Klavierbaues.* Wolfenbüttel and Berlin, 1937.

HIPKINS, Alfred J.: *Musical instruments, historic, rare and unique.* Edinburgh, 1888/London, 1921.

HIPKINS, Alfred J.: *A description and history of the pianoforte.* London, 1896.

HIRT, Franz Josef: *Meisterwerke des Klavierbaues.* Olten, 1955. Trs. M. Boehme-Raum as *Stringed keyboard instruments, 1440-1880.* Boston, 1968.

HUBBARD, Frank: *Three centuries of harpsichord making.* Harvard, 1967.

HUBERSON, G.: 'Manuel de l'accordeur de pianos' in *Encyclopédie Roret.* Paris, n.d.

JAMES, Philip: *Early keyboard instruments.* London, 1930/1960.

JANKO, Paul von: *Eine neue Klaviatur.* Vienna, 1886.

JONCKBLOET, W. J. A. and LAND, J. P. N.: *Musique et musiciens au XVIIe siècle.* Correspondence et oeuvres musicales de Constantin Huygens *(1596-1687).* Leyden, 1882.

JURAMIE, Ghislaine: *Histoire du piano.* Paris, 1948.

KINKELDEY, Otto: *Orgel und Klavier in der Musik des 16. Jahrhunderts.* Leipzig, 1910.

KINSKY, Georg: *Katalog des Musikhistorischen Museums von Wilhelm Heyer in Köln. Vol. 1, Besaitete Tasteninstrumente usw.* Cologne, 1910. The collection is now in the Karl-Marx Universität, Leipzig.

KÖHLER, H.: *Der Klavierunterricht.* Leipzig, 1868.

KREBS, K.: *Die besaiteten Klavierinstrumente bis zum Anfang des 17. Jahrhunderts.* Vierteljahrschrift für Musikwissenschaft VIII, Leipzig, 1892.

KREHBIEL, H. E.: *The pianoforte and its music.* London, 1911.

KULLAK, A. and NIEMANN, W.: *Ästhetik des Klavierspiels.* Berlin, 1905.

KÜTZING, C.: *Das Wissenschaftliche der Pianoforte Baukunst.* Bern, 1844.

LA BORDE, Jean-Benjamin de: *Le clavecin électrique.* Paris, 1761.

LANDOWSKA, Wanda: *La musique ancienne.* Paris, 1909.

LIGTVOET, A. W.: *European musical instruments in the Municipal Museum at the Hague.* 'S-gravenhage, n.d.

LUCIANI, S. A.: 'Clavichorde ou Clavecin?' *La revue musicale,* Vol. 15, No. 146. Paris, 1934.

LUITHLEN, Victor: *Der Eisenstädter Walterflügel.* Mozart-Jahrbuch, 1954. Salzburg, 1955.

LUITHLEN, Victor: *Katalog der Sammlung alter Musikinstrumente im Kunsthistorischen Museum, Wien.* Vienna, 1966.

MAHILLON, Victor-Charles: *Éléments d'acoustique.* Brussels, 1874.

MAHILLON, Victor-Charles: *Catalogue descriptif et analytique du Musée Instrumental du Conservatoire Royal de Musique de Bruxelles.* Ghent and Brussels, 1893-1922.

MARLIN, Jane: *Reminiscences of Morris Steinert.* New York, 1900.

MARMONTEL, A.: *Histoire du piano.* Paris, 1885.

MARPURG, Friedrich Wilhelm: *Antleitung zum Clavierspielen.* Berlin, 1765.

MATTHESON, Johann: *Das neu-eröffnete Orchestre.* Hamburg, 1713.
MÉRÉAUX, J. A. L. de: *Les Clavecinistes de 1637 à 1690.* Paris, 1867.
MERSENNE, Marin: *Harmonie universelle.* Paris, 1636-7.

NEF, Karl: *Clavicymbel und Clavichord.* Annuaire de la Bibliothèque musical Peters. Leipzig, 1904.
NEUPERT, Hanns: *Das Cembalo.* Kassel, 1951.
NEUPERT, Hanns: *Vom Musikstab zum modernen Klavier.* Berlin, 1952.
NEUPERT, J. C.: *Führer durch das musikhistorische Museum Neupert in Nürnberg.* Nürnberg, 1938.
NIEMANN, W.: *Virginalmusik.* Leipzig, 1919.
NORLIND, Tobias: *Systematik der Saiteninstrumente (Musikhistorisches Museum, Stockholm).* Stockholm, 1939.

PAGANELLI, Sergio (Trs. Anthony Rhodes): *Musical instruments from the Renaissance to the 19th century.* London, 1970.
PANNAIN, G.: *Le origini e lo sviluppo dell'arte pianistica in Italia dal 1500 al 1830.* Naples, 1917.
PAUL, Oscar: *Geschichte des Klaviers.* Leipzig, 1868.
PIERRE, Constant: *Les facteurs d'instruments de musique, les luthiers, et la facture instrumentale: précis historique.* Paris, 1893.
PIRRO, André: *Les Clavecinistes.* Paris, 1924.
PLEYEL: *La Salle Pleyel.* Paris, 1893.
POLS, André: *De Ruckers en de Klavierbouw en Vlaanderen.* Antwerp, 1942.
PONSICCHI, C.: *Il Pianoforte, sua origine e sviluppo.* Florence, 1876.
PONTÉCOULANT, A. de: *Organographie.* Paris, 1861.
PONTÉCOULANT, A. de: *Voyages d'un mélomane à travers l'Exposition Universelle.* Paris, 1862.
PRAETORIUS, Michael: *Syntagmatis musici.* Wolfenbüttel, 1619/Kassel, 1929.
PULITI, L.: *Cenni storici . . . della origine del pianoforte.* Atti dell'Accademia del R. Inst. Musicale di Firenze. Florence, 1874.

RAPIN, E.: *Histoire du piano et des pianistes.* Lausanne, 1904.
REVUE INTERNATIONALE DE MUSIQUE: *Volume spécial sur le piano, Vol. 1, No. 5-6.* Paris, 1939.
RIMBAULT, Edward Francis: *The pianoforte, its origin, progress and construction.* London, 1860.

RIPIN, Edwin M.: *Keyboard instruments. Studies in keyboard organology.* Edinburgh, 1971.

ROES, P.: *Essai sur la technique du piano.* Paris, 1935.

ROUGNON, P.: *Pianos et pianistes.* Paris, 1895.

RÜCK, Ulrich: *Mozarts Hammerflügel erbaute Anton Walter, Wien.* Mozart-Jahrbuch, 1955, Salzburg, 1956.

RUSSELL, Raymond: *The harpsichord since 1800.* Proceedings of the R.M.A., Vol. LXXXII, 1956.

RUSSELL, Raymond: *Catalogue of the Benton Fletcher Collection at Fenton House, Hampstead, London.* London, 1957.

RUSSELL, Raymond: *The harpsichord and clavichord.* London, 1959/1973.

RUSSELL, Raymond: *Catalogue of musical instruments in the Victoria and Albert Museum, London, Vol. 1, Keyboard instruments.* London, 1968.

RUSSELL, Raymond: *The Russell Collection and other early keyboard instruments in Saint Cecilia's Hall, Edinburgh.* Edinburgh, 1968.

RUTH-SOMMER, Hermann: *Alte Musikinstrumente.* Berlin, 1920.

SACHS, Curt: *Reallexicon der Musikinstrumente.* Berlin, 1913.

SACHS, Curt: *Handbuch der Musikinstrumentenkunde.* Leipzig, 1920.

SACHS, Curt: *Sammlung alter Musikinstrumente bei der Staatlichen Hochschule für Musik zu Berlin. Beschreibender Katalog.* Berlin, 1922.

SACHS, Curt: *Das Klavier.* Berlin, 1923.

SACHS, Curt: *The history of musical instruments.* New York, 1940/London, 1942.

SCHAEFFNER, A.: 'Clavecin', art. in *Encyclopédie de la Musique et Dictionnaire du Conservatoire.* Paris, n.d.

SCHAFHAÜTL, K. E. von: *Die Pianofortebaukunst der Deutschen.* Munich, 1855.

SCHLOSSER, Julius: *Die Sammlung alter Musikinstrumente im Kunsthistorischen Museum, Wien.* Vienna, 1920.

SEIFFERT, Max: *Geschichte der Klaviermusik, Vol. 1.* Leipzig, 1899.

SKINNER, William: *The Belle Skinner Collection of old musical instruments at Holyoke, Massachusetts.* Springfield, Mass., 1933.

STELLFELD, J. A.: *Bronnen tot de geschiedenis der Antwerpsche clavecimbel - en orgelbouwers in de XVIe en XVII eeuwen.* Antwerp, 1942.

STRAETEN, Edmond van der: *La musique aux Pay Bas.* Brussels, 1867-88.

SUMNER, W. L.: *The pianoforte.* London, 1966.

THON, C. F. G.: *Abhandlung über Klavier-Saiteninstrumenten.* Weimar, 1836.

VILLANIS, L. A.: *L'Arte del clavicembalo.* Turin, 1901.

VILLANIS, L. A.: *L'Arte del pianoforte in Italia.* Turin, 1909.

VIRDUNG, Sebastian: *Musica getutscht und auszgezogen.* Basel, 1511/ Berlin, 1882/Kassel, 1931.

WALLNER, L.: *De la mathésis musicale.* Brussels, 1891.

WINTERNITZ, Emanuel: *Keyboard instruments in the Métropolitan Museum of Art.* New York, 1961.

WINTERNITZ, Emanuel: *Musical instruments of the Western World.* London, 1966.

WELCKER VON GONTERSHAUSEN, Heinrich: *Der Klavierbau.* Frankfurt, 1870.

ZUCKERMANN, Wolfgang Joachim: *The modern harpsichord.* New York/London, 1970.

INDEX

149

153